*The kingdom of heaven is like a grain of mustard seed.
When it has grown it becomes a tree, so that the birds
of the air come and make nests in its branches.*

Canterbury
MUSTARD SEEDS

A Selecton of Homilies from the regular Sunday
Eucharist and Shared Meal at Canterbury House,
University of Wyoming, Laramie

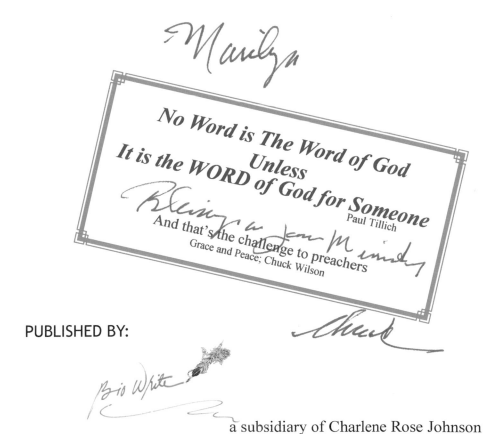

No Word is The Word of God
Unless
It is the WORD of God for Someone
Paul Tillich

And that's the challenge to preachers
Grace and Peace; Chuck Wilson

PUBLISHED BY:

Bio Write

a subsidiary of Charlene Rose Johnson

Published by BioWrite
A company owned by Charlene R. Johnson
14971 SE 107th Ave, Summerfield, FL 34491

It is the policy of BioWrite to print the books we publish on acid-free paper and in the best environmental methods we know.

Wilson, Charles R.
    Canterbury Mustard Seeds: Charles R. Wilson

ISBN: 978-0-692-01227-7

Printed in the United States of America

First Edition

Photography and Book Design by Charlene R. Johnson
www.BioWrite.com

DEDICATION

In 1981 Lynne and I published a little book on the subject of theology, creativity and surprise. Its focus was church planning; its emphasis was on creativity as a playful enterprise and it supported this emphasis by characterizing God as a playful creator.

We characterized ourselves (like Abraham) as Sojourners in the Land of Promise. That journey ended when Lynne became ill in Advent, 2005 and died in January '06.

This volume is dedicated to the memories of that journey and to my colleague, companion and mate, my perennial delight and joy on the way.

LYNNE ELIZABETH WILSON   (1944 – 2006)

".. . and (Abraham) went out not knowing where he was to go. By Faith he sojourned in the land of promise . . ."

Hebrews 11:8

TABLE OF CONTENTS

FOREWORD

Charles R. Wilson, Chaplain

Canterbury House is open every day the University is in session. Students and others can drop in to study, hang out, watch TV, listen to recorded music, do a laundry, take a nap–or some combination of the above. It is usually a quiet, hassle free environment, a place one could to retreat to, "To be still then and know that I am God."

The facility can also be scheduled for formally sponsored group activities that are compatible with our social and educational purposes. It is frequently used by diocesan or campus related groups as a convenient place for meetings and meals, and hospitality for other groups is considered part of our campus ministry.

Two apartments on a separate floor are normally let to students under an agreement that they will look after certain custodial services as part of their rent. The Canterbury House facility and the community normally occupying it are formally recognized as campus programs by the University, and as such, we have our faculty advisor providing formal linkage between Canterbury House and the University. The Faculty Advisor during most of my tenure was Elizabeth (Beth) A. Hardin, V. P. for Administration. Beth and I became a fairlyeffective leadership team during our years together at the university and Canterbury House flourished. It was Beth's suggestion that we call this collection of homilies Mustard Seeds.

This was my first experience in campus ministry. I retired from part-time parochial work and private practice in June 1999. My wife Lynne had been called as Wyoming's Ministries Development Coordinator a year earlier and was already living in Laramie. So, I joined her. For the first three years I did some interim work in small congregations in the southern part of the state. Then the

Chaplaincy position opened up right in my backyard, and I was getting tired of the driving. So, I took it on as a volunteer. The demands were modest; preach and preside at the Sunday afternoon Eucharist. Then hang around for a meal prepared by students or (on occasion) by members of the cathedral congregation.

So, I started pondering what kind of preaching menu would be appropriate for these young adults. I soon learned what Beth already knew. They are like sponges. You can't preach over their heads, they catch it all. You don't have to protect them from contemporary social issues; they are already on top of that stuff. Those bright young minds invite challenge, confrontation, deep thinking. Don't try to smooth it over, cover it up, or make it taste better. Honest, straight-forward Biblical scholarship doesn't scare them a bit.

I discovered that these youngsters had, for the most part, a good grounding in the faith. They had grown up in the church. As those things go, they were theologically astute and Biblically literate. (I felt an overwhelming sense of gratitude for those parish based teachers who had brought them this far. At least I had something to build on.) Of course we did run into those who did not have such a background, but, we had a bunch of evangelists on hand who were their contemporaries, spoke their language and were willing to reach out – they could, and did, cover it.

So, I began to plot my course. It was a very freeing experience. All I had to do in my preaching was be as direct, honest and straightforward as I could be and deliver the best theology and Biblical scholarship at my command. In all this I would seek some theological balance in the overall menu and try to advance them in keeping with their basic intellectual growth. They don't come to the university to study grade school math, nor (I reasoned) to color Sunday school pictures. So, on September 7th, 2003, I launched into it. Our relationships deepened as we all relaxed into a very informal routine of sharing the leadership at the Sunday liturgy, and the cooking and serving afterward. Some twelve or so months later I began to feel that a theme was emerging and discussed it with Beth. She felt it too and identified it as "mustard seeds."

September 9, 2003

WHAT IS A CONGREGATION FOR?

First Homily at Canterbury

What is a congregation for? Well first, I suppose we should establish that Canterbury House is indeed a congregation. It is not a parish. But it is a Christian community and we do a lot of the things that congregations do. So for now I'm going to treat Canterbury House as one of the congregations of The Diocese of Wyoming. But what is any congregation for? Congregations maintain lists of members, publish catalogues of programs and services, plan and oversee budgets and contributions of members, take part in diocesan and ecumenical affairs, maintain buildings and grounds, host activities of outside groups, teach classes, sponsor corporate worship and a whole range of other activities. But what is it all for?

I'll give you my answer to that question. After all, we should have some sense of what we are about now as we embark on this journey together. I'll simply lay my cards out so you can see how I understand what it is that we are up to. From here on, as far as I'm concerned, everything we do should be understood in the light of the basic purpose of Canterbury House.

I understand that a congregation is the support base for the ministries of its members in the world. Ministries of its members, not the ministry of its ordained people only. In the world, not primarily church stuff. This means, of course, that we are all ministers and that our baptismal covenant is our common guide. So, we will keep that before us as we go. The question then becomes, how do we do that? How does a congregation address this purpose of maintaining itself as a support base for the ministries of its members in the world? Well there are many ways to get at this, but I'm going to sketch out four key things that we must be about in order to be effective on our mission.

Corporate worship, of course is a central activity of a congregation. It's a huge subject, so in order to say something worth-while, I'll focus on a piece of the liturgy often thought of as an unimportant add-on; the offertory. I suppose if you were to ask most people just what the purpose of the offering is, they would explain it in terms of the need for financial support of the church. Actually there is some truth to that. But it is near the bottom of my list. The primary need that is served in that part of the liturgy we call the offertory is our need to give. We simply have to spend ourselves somehow in this world to discover our own worth. Or to slightly paraphrase, how will we know what our lives are worth in this world until we see what we spend them on? Our lives are worth precisely what we spend them on. This is called ministry, or "ministry in Christ" and we address it in terms of our baptismal vows.

So, think of all the things you spend your life on. Most of you are students, so you spend a lot of your time in study. That can be seen as an investment in your future ministry; but along the way there is lots of opportunity to minister as you study; to be a good companion with other members of the academic and the Christian communities, to reach out, to lend a helping hand. A lot of you are involved in sports; lots of room to be a good neighbor (or to minister) there too. Some of you have some earning capa-bility. Sharing with worthy causes is probably limited for most of you, but it is an area to be examined.

Now, liturgically, this is represented in the offertory. That bread and wine is our flesh and blood. Think of it as your spend-ing of yourself through the week just past. The contribution of our lives is in that offering. Feel it heaped up in those offering basins: your life, the good and the not so good, heaped up, car-ried to the altar where it is presented to the Lord, blessed, sanc-tified, made holy. The bread and wine is then received by us as flesh and blood of the Lord as we live in him and he in us. No, the offertory doesn't just represent our church support, it represents how we are spending our lives.

A second key activity of a congregation is pastoral care; look-ing out for one another. I generally think of this as consisting of two parts; both are very important and both require quality attention. One I'll call general pastoral care. By this I mean the normal things we do simply to build and maintain community. For example the Sunday afternoon meal we share. There is a lot of community building going on there, not just in the eating of the food and visiting around the table, but also in the preparations required, the clean up after eating, planning and scheduling things. If you have any doubts about the high quality of this time we spend together, join me out here in the hall sometime while the after-dinner clean up is going on in the kitchen and listen to the "buzz." High quality "buzz" is a very good indicator of the significance of community-building under way.

The other part of this I'll call special pastoral care. Here I mean the kind of looking after one another when something special is going on in someone's life; special times of joy and celebration, special times of grieving and questioning. Many of these are liturgical occasions in the life of the congregation: weddings, funerals, baptisms, house blessings, etc. We also have illnesses including hospitalization, surgery, accidents; then there are anniversaries, birthdays and other things to celebrate. I think that we in the Episcopal Church are especially good at pastoral care. It is rooted in our theology. We know that we are all sinners. A lot of Christians will readily admit that, but we live it. We know we are sinners, so we don't have to play games about it. We don't have to pretend otherwise. We simply assume it, and that saves us from pretense and it keeps us out of the judging business. It saves a lot of time and frees us to be genuine pastors to one another and to our neighbors; a great plus in our communion.

A third set of ministries can be thought of as educational. We need to teach our youngest folk the Bible stories. They can come to understand their meanings later. But in my opinion, the stories come first. Once they have the stories, we have something to build on. Later on we can help them see that "the stories" are really "One Story" and that the themes in the One Story are themes in their stories also. Resurrection, crucifixion, exodus, and so on are themes in everybody's story. By the time they are in high school they should be able to recognize those themes in the daily news, in the experiences of their friends and in their own lives.

Christian education is not just for kids, it's for all ages, Conformation classes, special advanced courses for adults, training for special ministries (readers, Eucharistic ministers, choir and a host of others). We live in a world of highly educated specialists and we simply cannot be satisfied sending adult Christians into the world with a Sunday school education. Furthermore, there are scads of materials out there today; Education For Ministry (EFM) a seminary extension course has been around for more than twenty five years, and more courses are available all the time. Add to that the fact that we live in a diocesan environment where everybody's ministry is valued and supported. That doesn't mean that just any ole body can stand up in front of the congregation and preach. But it does mean that with proper preparation there is not much that any of you will be precluded from. The name of that 'proper preparation' is education.

Finally, I'll comment briefly on authentication, which is both the easiest to provide and the easiest to neglect. You know what the word 'authority' means. Well when it comes to ministering in Christ's name in the world we all do that under the authority of our baptism. Recall the words spoken by the congregation at the end of the baptismal service. The officiant first says, "Let us welcome the newly-baptized." The congregation responds with two sentences. The first is indeed a 'welcome.' "We receive you into the household of God." The second is more like marching orders, "Confess the faith of Christ crucified, proclaim his resurrection, and share with us in his eternal priesthood." Or, to paraphrase, "OK so you are baptized; what are you standing around for? Get out there in the world to witness and minister in Christ's name."

So, our ministries are authorized! But they need sustained support. Earlier in the service, at the end of the baptismal vows, the officiant addresses the congregation; "Will you who witness these vows do all in your power to support these persons in their life in Christ?" and we all answer "We will." No one is expected to journey alone. We have all vowed to support one another with "all in our power."

It was many years ago while I was serving as a volunteer priest in a fairly large church in eastern Pennsylvania, that the importance of authentication really clicked in my head. This church was promoting mutual ministry which was why I joined them.

They were well along in the development of mutual or total ministry, with laity involved in all kinds of things unheard of in the rest of the diocese. They already had numerous workshops which I eventually got involved in.

Anyway there was an engineer there, Ed, who was on the faculty of the local college. Ed was an authenticator par excellence. And I came to experience Ed's ministry of authentication first hand and with some frequency. If I were the preacher for the day, Ed would likely approach me quietly after the service, put a hand on my shoulder and say something like, "Chuck that was a solid message. We are certainly lucky to have you as part of this parish." And it wasn't only preaching and it wasn't only me. I started watching this guy and he frequently approached others in the congregation with a quiet word of "Thanks, you do that so well." It wasn't flattery and it wasn't phony. It was just that where most of us might admire another's performance, but let it go (no need to embarrass anyone) Ed moved on it. And it was contagious.

Others caught on and soon it was common to see authentication solidly at work in this church: a hug here, a quiet word of appreciation there. It was not just for contributions to church activities. It was a small town. Members knew what was going in each other's lives in the larger community. Authentication followed members in their various ministries in the world, and that's what a congregation is for; the support of the ministries of the members in the world.

That's my vision of what a congregation is for-to provide support services for its members in their ministries in the world. We can sum up those support services in four words; Worship, Pastoral support, Education and Authentication. I'm sure you can quickly see how the four depend on one another. If one part is missing or inadequate, the whole suffers. In fact, the whole is missing. Anyway, that should give you a fairly good picture of what I'll be working on while with you. I'm looking forward to it. May God bless us on this journey together.

FLATLAND

Plane Geometry

Our world is full of wonder, and rich experiences. We are so much a part of it we're inclined to think of it as the real world. We can take off in a plane, fly across the country at 40,000 feet, then land, and think nothing of it.

We can dive off a board into the pool, swim along under water, come to the surface and paddle along some more. We can hop and skip and jump rope; go up escalators and steps and elevators–and come back down again. We can move up and down about as easily as we can move left or right, and hardly notice it. We even talk about the "ups" and "downs" of life as having something to do with good fortune or bad as these random events come upon us in life's experiences.

But things are different in Flatland. In Flatland those metaphors would communicate nothing, up and down. People there wouldn't understand what that meant at all.

Flatland is a world of two dimensions. The people in Flatland never experience the rain or the snow falling. They never look up to see the sun, stars or clouds. They never look down at their feet; they haven't any such experiences. There is no up or down; just right or left.

The people of Flatland come in a variety of shapes. There are triangles and squares, hexagons and pentagons and all kinds of figures. But, of course, the natives of Flatland wouldn't understand those figures as we do. That is to say, they wouldn't experience them as we do because, after all, we can look **down** at a table or floor and see such forms. They can't do that. They can only look horizontally. We can readily distinguish between a triangle and a square, but in Flatland it is a little more difficult. Looking horizontally, all you see are the corners and angles.

Now the people of Flatland have some sense of these shapes. They realize that some people have three angles and three sides. So they have figured out what a triangle is; they just can't visualize one as we do. And they know about squares; people with four sides and four angles. And so it is they have learned how to "size up" each other as they go about their business. They can make a fairly quick estimate of the relative "importance" of the people they meet by taking note of the number of sides and the number of angles you can see from one vantage point. For, you see, the more sides and angles you have, the greater the esteem one is accorded in Flatland.

The simple and menial tasks tend to be delegated to triangles and squares. Philosophers, doctors and lawyers, for example might have upwards of thirty or forty sides. The mayor of Flatland, who is an attorney, is held in highest regard of all. It has been estimated that she has nearly a hundred sides and angles. However, nobody knows for sure because no one has been brazen enough to actually walk around her and count them. In any case, she's almost a circle. Oh yes, I should mention that in Flatland there are no circles.

The Flatlanders have a sense of what a circle might be because if you got so many sides and so many angles, with the sides so short and the angles so slight you might eventually get to the point where there would be no angles at all; just one smooth line all the way around; and that would be a circle. For the people of Flatland that would represent wholeness, perfection. It would be like having a god in their midst. But, of course, human nature, being what it is, no one really expects to see a circle. They just don't occur. People aren't that good.

The people in Flatland live much as we do; except for being limited to two dimensions. They come and go. They work at their various trades. They raise families and live in houses. The houses of Flatlanders are just a series of lines that enclose spaces. With our way of seeing things we wouldn't see much more than a "floor plan." For them it's "corners and sides" again, but they have openings where they can go in and out as they wish; and they have rooms for various purposes.

Getting married in Flatland is sometimes a problem. The young people always aspire to marry up. You know what I mean: to find a mate who has more sides and is held in higher regard. Of course, the reason for this is the hope that they will have children who are better than they are. At best it's a risk. Most children turn out to be very much like the parents.

Well, that's Flatland. Our story starts when this particular Flatlander is just getting home from work. We'll just call him "Square." Square comes around the corner of his house, over to the doorway, passes on through the door and into one of the larger rooms. All of a sudden, there, right before his eyes is a circle; and not only a circle, but a huge circle, too large to have come through the doorway. Square is just about frightened out of his wits. He doesn't know whether to turn and run screaming, or to fall down and worship the thing, or to . . . Well, he screws up his courage, stands there with his heart pounding, looks at the circle and says, "Well who are you and where did you come from? And how did you get through that door?"

Circle responds, "I just thought I'd drop by for a visit. I come from another world. I come from a three-dimensional world. And I didn't come through your door." Square, still shaking, challenged, "What are you talking about? There are only two dimensions. What do you mean, a three-dimensional world? And how did you get in here? What kind of nonsense are you giving me?"

Circle tries to explain a little more: "You see, I'm not a circle; I'm really a sphere; a ball-and the reason you see me as a circle is because you live in this two-dimensional Flatland and, of course, a cross section of a sphere, as anyone knows, is a circle. So, all **you** see is a circle, but really I'm a sphere. I didn't come through your door, you see; I just came into your plane of existence. I can move in and out of it at will.

Square, beginning to relax, but still completely baffled said,

"Whatever are you babbling about? I never heard of such non-sense! What can you possibly be talking about?"

Circle was at his wits' end; he didn't know how to explain all this to Square. Finally Circle said, "Here, I'll show you. I'll move in and out of Flatland and you will be able to see what that does to a cross section of a sphere." As Square watched, Circle got smaller and smaller, till he all but disappeared; then he got larger and larger and even larger than he was before as Sphere moved back into the plane of Flatland. Square had never seen anything shrink or grow like that. "Now do you see what I mean?" asked Circle.

"It must be a trick, or magic," said Square. "I just don't have any idea of what you're trying to describe to me and I don't believe what I just saw."

"Well, it's plain to see that you're stuck in your two dimen-sions. You really can't see the possibility of other worlds. So, if you'll come with me, we'll go visit some of them." Square was ready to do that all right; his curiosity was up. "First," said Circle, "I'll take you to a world of one dimension."

So they came to a world of one dimension. It was a long line. The people in that world were just dashes and dots on a line; everybody in a row. The dashes and dots were racing along, making noises like horns tooting. Nobody knew where they were going; no one knew where they had come from, but everyone was in a rush to move along the line like traffic on a freeway, however nobody could pass any one else. There was just one dimension. Square looked at it and said, "Oh, how sad. What a terrible way to live. I'm so glad that I live in Flatland."

"Well, you haven't seen anything yet. Let me show you a world of no dimensions." So they went to a world of no dimen-sions, and there was a single dot that kept saying, "I am, I am, I am, I am." But it wasn't anything at all and there wasn't anything else either, and it didn't go anywhere. It was just a pulsating dot that said, "I am."

"Oh that's pathetic. I'm sure glad I live in Flatland where we can go places and do things."

"Well, come on," said Circle, "I might as well show you my world which is a world of three dimensions." So, they went to the world of three dimensions where all of a sudden, Square discovered that he was a Cube. He looked around and saw cones and pyramids, and hills and valleys, and he could jump up and down and run around. He could look behind things and over things, and he saw what a sphere was. "So, that's what Circle was talking about; a sphere, how lovely." And he had more fun looking at all the sizes and shapes and trying to imagine what the people back in Flatland would be like if they were here in a three-dimensional world. He was so excited. Finally, he said, "Well, come on! Let's go visit another world. I want to see the world of four dimensions."

"There's no world of four dimensions, just three!" But Square insisted, "No, I want to see the world of four dimensions; then I'd like to see one with five and ten, and maybe twenty dimensions. Come on. Take me to some more worlds. I want to see what I would be in a world of more dimensions."

"You're crazy," said Circle. "How can there be more than three dimensions? That's all there are; this is the real world!"

"I thought two dimensions was all there were, and you proved that there could be three. Now I know you and me in three dimensions. There must be four dimensions somewhere, and there are probably ten or a dozen or even more. I want to go visit some of those other worlds, to know us in those worlds."

Circle tried to make him understand that it was impossible to have more than three dimensions. But they went on arguing and arguing, and I suppose they're still arguing about it. At least that's all the story I know. And, of course, it is, after all, a make believe land, this "Flatland."

We live in the **real** world, you and I, where we can skip rope and jump and hop and run around. We live in the real world of beauty, love, joy . . . and of tragedy. Yes, the real world of AIDS, weapons of mass destruction, cancer; the real world where children can die in accidents or even starve to death.

This is the real world; three dimensions, or four if you want to be scientific and include time. The real world where the first are first and the last, last. Where the master is boss and the servant, servant. Where people don't walk on water, virgins don't have babies and if you want to feed five thousand people you order up a freight carload of bread.

But what if . . . what if there **were** other worlds? Worlds of six or ten or twenty dimensions? We wouldn't know about it anyway! How could we? How could we discover it? Locked in our three-dimensional world, how could we experience it? How could we come to believe it?

Well, I suppose somebody would just have to come from there . . . and tell us about it!

UNION

And the Two Become One

This past week Lynne and I celebrated our 21st wedding anniversary. It wasn't a terribly intimate celebration since she was over in Cheyenne looking after this year's diocesan convention and I was holed up in Laramie recovering from elbow surgery. However such occasions are not to be ignored. So, before leaving for Cheyenne, she presented me with this anniversary present. It is called "Canadian" (A Canada Goose in flight) #7 of 30 and signed by the sculpture Richard Tucker.

A few weeks ago we took some time off for a tour of the Black Hills. The hotel that served as our base of operations was featuring a resident artist who was working on a charging Rocky Mountain sheep in the lobby as he visited with hotel guests. Over those few days we became quite close to Richard and his wife as we shared interests artistic and theological. (He had once been a Methodist cleric.) Anyway, Lynne managed to secretly purchase this example of his artistic talent and smuggle it home.

It is such times: anniversaries, birthdays and miscellaneous other occasions that provide opportunity for couples -- at least this couple -- to back off for a moment, in a reflective mood and with a deep sense of gratitude, and recognize the wonderful miracle and reality of these words from Genesis: Therefore a man leaves his father and his mother and clings to his wife, and they become one flesh. Don't lose that. In a good marriage we come to know the truth, that even with mutual respect for each other's personal identity and character, the two seem to become one, more whole and complete, unit of humanity.

The point has, on more than one occasion, placed me in some challenging pastoral situations. I'll recount a couple of them.

Years ago a woman came to me with some troubling marital problems. I knew this woman and her husband and the little girl who was part of the scene very well. It seemed to me that this was a strong family situation. All three were very active in the church, and the church community loved and supported them. This was the second marriage for her, and the little girl was hers by her first husband.

Then came the turning point. With great anticipation they were about to take custody of her older child, a son, about thirteen. This lad had been terribly abused by his father, which is why the authorities had originally held on to him for awhile. Anyway the woman's new husband took on this challenge with what I thought was uncommon courage, hope and confidence. It soon became clear however, that the youngster had been too severely damaged.

I helped the couple get him into St. Francis Home for Children in Kansas. However the staff there couldn't do anything with him and he came back home where he proceeded to abuse everybody around him. At one point his distraught mother came to me and cried out, "But Chuck, what am I supposed to do? After all, my son comes first!" And I replied forcefully, "Absolutely Not! You have it backwards. You stood before God and family and friends and vowed that your first loyalty henceforth would be to your husband. And that's the way it has to be. It won't work any other way. Get your marriage back together first. Then the two of you, together, figure out what, if anything, you can do about your son." But she couldn't do that, and the marriage broke up.

I've since lost track of them; but my best guess is that the son is, probably in prison somewhere. The husband, could very well be in a new, one hopes, more promising marriage. The little girl is no doubt on her own by now. And the woman is probably a bruised, sad old lady struggling somewhere to make ends meet, because, having lost track of her priorities, she threw away a perfectly good marriage.

The second story revolves around similar issues: Again it was the woman who approached me. I knew her very well. I knew her husband less well as he was less active in the church; but I did know him and liked him. They had two children; a pre-teen (at the time) daughter, and a younger son. It looked to me like there was a great deal of strength and affection in this young family. Anyway, she came to me after church one Sunday and indicated that she wanted to talk. I quickly saw that it was a pastoral matter, so we sought a quiet place where we could visit without interruption. It turned out that her mother had moved in with the family and, while things were peaceful so far, she was concerned for the long-term stresses that would inevitably crop up; little annoyances that could pile up.

So, we reviewed her wedding vows, reflected on two becoming one flesh; and the fact that there could be no question about where the priorities were, etc. So I told her to go home and discuss these things with her husband so he would not be surprised at unfolding developments. Then I told her to confront her mother, gently, lovingly, but firmly; share her worries, and offer to work with her mom to resolve her living arrangements.

I didn't hear from her again for some six weeks. (She was in church every Sunday, but didn't bring it up. Since it is not my practice to "own" the issue after a single session, I didn't bring it up either.) Sometime later she approached me again. Once more we sought a quiet place where we could visit. She explained that she had followed through on the plan. And she was so grateful for how understanding and caring her mother had been. Together they had worked out options and in short order her mother was comfortably settled in private quarters. Furthermore, the various members of this extended family were all in a good place with regard to each other, and, more importantly, she no longer felt that her nuclear family was faced with undue stress. I ran into her some years later. She again thanked me for my counsel, indicating that things were still going well with all, and that she was now serving on the vestry.

So, my friends, hang onto the wisdom and wonder and the priorities implied in the words, "Therefore a man leaves his father and his mother and clings to his wife, and they become one flesh."

But we must also examine another side of these matters. And for that we turn to the Gospel: The Pharisees came to Jesus "to test him." Is it lawful for a man to divorce his wife? This is a male dominated society. Therefore the rights and privileges of males receive primary consideration. Jesus rightfully comes back with the hard line response "NO!" But consider the times; what's a divorced woman to do? She can't become a teacher or a nurse, or a bank teller, or a computer programmer; and if she remarries the neighbors will claim she is living in adultery. About all she can do is take to the streets. Meanwhile, the guy is free to take up his life anew. For the most of history, our church has adhered to the hard line response to this question (The R.C.Curch still does). However in more recent times new realities and new insights have been influencing policies and practices, and the strict hard line is no longer appropriate.

Studies have shown that in all periods of history and in all parts of the world in those cultures where women are oppressed, can't own property, have no independent wealth and have precious few rights of any kind, divorce is very rare. Look at conservative Islamic countries today. Or look at our own country pre-World War II; days of the diversified family farm. You had one cash crop: milk, beef, corn, wheat; the woman got the egg money. There were lots of kids to cover lots of chores. That unit was almost self-sufficient. There was, typically, a large vegetable garden, an orchard, pigs, chickens, sometimes sheep, goats and so on. You canned fruits and vegetables all summer, smoked ham and bacon in the fall in order to have plenty for the table through the winter. Now, in that scene there's no way out. If the wife wants to leave, will she take half the farm with her?

Not only that, but in those days there were tremendous social pressures against divorce. I recall seeing many families terribly dysfunctional; couldn't divorce, couldn't stand living together. To complicate things there very likely were members of the larger family hanging around as part of that household; elderly parents, uncles, aunts etc. So, you might see for example, the husband and wife screaming at and cursing each other all through breakfast. Later, he's off to the barn and fields, and she to the cellar (laundry) and hen house; people hopelessly trapped in impossible situations. Then, tremendous social and economic change. The standard of living soared. Jobs and careers opened for women. Women's liberation! Incredible changes and we are still in them. But we are a stronger, more liberated society because of those changes. Which also means we have become a culture in which women have many more rights and opportunities than that American world of 60 -70 years ago. And with that, divorce is much more common and acceptable.

I want to make one more point in this context. It used to be assumed that divorce equated with a "failed" marriage. I challenge that assumption and suggest another way of looking at it, offering my own experience as an illustration. I was married to my first wife for over thirty years. For those thirty years we looked after each other "for richer, for poorer, in sickness and in health." We raised four children who are today responsible contributors to society in their unique ways. They are very close to each other, to their parents and step parents, and others who are part of this extended family. I don't consider that a "failed" marriage. It ended earlier than originally intended. Neither do I consider that an unforgivable sin. We exercised one of the very tough options we have today for resolving difficult relationship problems we can sometimes find ourselves in.

We have examined two sides of the marriage/divorce issue which is big in our times. Questions surrounding these things will certainly confront you at some point. I have tried to be open, honest, direct and (I hope) helpful. I hope you will remember both sides: First the beautiful words from Genesis which I now paraphrase to set them in more inclusive language: "Therefore, a couple leave their parents and cling to one another, and the two become one flesh." Second, the hard line of Jesus which I have suggested as the best way to go, given the incredible inequality of women and men in those times. But times change and we must rethink these things for our time and culture. I pray that if, your choice is marriage, you will find many rich blessings as you and your partner grow together. On the other hand, if sometime out there, you find yourself in an abusive or otherwise bad scene, you will know that you rightfully have options and can use them responsibly. Blessings on you all!

SERVANTHOOD

Authority in the Church

What do you think? Did Jesus actually say that last part, or is that Mark's spin on something Jesus said? I'll read it again:

Whoever wishes to become great among you must be your servant;

Whoever wishes to be first among you must be slave of all.

This is what the scholars refer to as a parallelism; two lines that say essentially the same thing. The second line repeats the sense of the first in slightly different words. It is a very common literary or poetic device in Hebrew Scriptures. You'll find them all through the Book of Psalms and elsewhere in the Old Testament. However that doesn't tell us much about who wrote this one. So, let's come at it another way.

Can you believe that Mother Teresa was servant of all because she aspired to greatness? If we put it that way it doesn't come out right, does it? You can probably accept that Mother Teresa was servant of all because in God's love she was compelled to seek and to serve Christ in all persons. That the world ascribed greatness to her is incidental, unnecessary and unsought from her point of view.

I'll tell you who I could ascribe those words to. In the 50s there were two very popular speakers and writers. You may have heard of them. One was Dale Carnegie who went around the country teaching thousands how to be successful in the business world. His best selling book was How to win Friends and Influence People. I was never a fan but I was involved in many management workshops where his approach was touted. I believe it still is, as I can still see evidence of it. What I didn't like about the guy was what I was reading into the title. (I did read the book, by the way) The book title sounded to me like How to win Friends in order to Use People. I saw it as manipulative. His followers would deny that, I should hasten to add. "You can't fake it" they would say. "It has to be genuine–not just an act." And some of his disciples were very good at that. However I still tripped over the means/ends problem.

Norman Vincent Peale was a Dale Carnegie in church guise. He was pastor of one of New York City's huge churches, wrote a regular column, preached to a packed church every Sunday and so on. His sermon was always the same: lead a good Christian life and you will be showered with blessings (meaning money, success, happiness, the world's goods, etc.). I once stopped in to browse through the books in a large department store's book section. I was amused to see a huge stack of Norman Vincent Peale's latest book, not in the religion department, but in a section devoted to "successful living," Dale Carnegie's section. Very appropriate organizing, in my opinion. Of the two, I thought Carnegie was the more genuine and honest. People attracted to his courses wanted to be "successful," Peale was simply a lousy theologian. People attracted to his services also wanted to be liked, successful and so on, but they wouldn't have understood Mother Teresa, and Peale should have.

I'll come back to the authorship question directly. But first let's take a look at how authority really does work in the church. For that I'll pick up on Matthew's understanding of authority. According to Matthew all authority is God's authority. It is not expressed in orders, declarations, demands, delegations or rules. Authority is expressed in actions. It works something like this: An individual who is free (not under orders, demands or rules) hears the call and responds in faith and in freedom. The resulting action is an expression of God's authority. I'll illustrate: During the years Lynne and I were based in Colorado, we frequented a certain book and church supply shop. It was not superior service that kept us there but the fact that they had no competition to speak of. We basically liked the people, but they worked under such close supervision it was no fun dealing with them. For example, on one occasion when I was in the shop I noticed a display of personal sized Prayer Books on sale: 40% off. How fortunate I thought, (I was in the market for one as a gift). There was a stack of red leather-bound books on the left and right next to them, a stack of blue. The sale sign was on the red books but appeared to apply to both. Just to make sure, I called a clerk and asked. The clerk strained her neck to check the display, and finally said "Oh, I don't know, I'll have to go ask Keith."

Another time I had bought a book and the thing fell apart on me-bad binding! So I returned it within a month, (different clerk) and asked for credit. She examined it apprehensively and concluded, "Oh, I'll have to go get Keith." And so it is in this shop when anything out of the ordinary comes up. Consider for a minute the atmosphere in such a workplace. The clerks are tied to strict rules, no leeway to decide on their own; everybody up-tight. What kind of spirit is guiding things in this place?

Contrast that setting with this one. For the past four years I've been doing supervised physical therapy in a gym in a clinic near here. For the first six months I couldn't tell who was in charge; and, being a management consultant and curious about such things, I finally had to ask. (There are some twenty staff members involved). Having received an answer, I began to pay more attention to how things worked in this facility.

Apart from the CEO, there are physical therapists, assistants, and two or three classes of trainees. The PTs are clearly in charge of servicing their assigned patients, however the assignments are quite flexible from one day to the next. The PTs freely elicit assistance from other staff personnel as needed and as others are available. I've never seen any evidence of a chain of command other than this or, for that matter, of anyone "ordering" anyone else. At staff meetings everybody sits in a big circle in the gym. The chair moves around, individual to individual, depending on the evolving agenda. The casual observer will have no idea of who is in charge. One might wonder what kind of spirit is guiding things here?

Now to draw the contrast: I would characterize the actions of personnel in the bookstore as routine, cautious, unimaginative, orderly, dull and controlled; the actions of the staff in the gym as free, loving, creative, risky, responsible and out of control. In other words (and this is the authority point) the actions of the bookstore folk showed no evidence of authority whatsoever-void-empty. The actions of the gym personnel were loaded with dynamic, creative authority throughout.

I'll point out another contrast. In the bookstore it was the word of Keith that counted-nobody else's mattered. In the gym, you get the sense that anyone who speaks to you, from the CEO to the lowest ranking aid, speaks the Word of the gym. So, again, the bookstore; void of authority. The gym, loaded with authority, for everyone there speaks as "one with authority." And the difference is the Spirit that is guiding things.

So, is it a direct quote of Jesus' or Mark's spin on it? I think that Jesus would feel quite at home in the gym environment. Mark, on the other hand would find the spirit of the bookstore more familiar. Actions in the gym would feel, to him, unstructured, out of control. I think the quote represents Mark's spin on Jesus' words and, probably, Mark's background in structures of authority.

Now, I'll put two more questions before you:

Where does the Holy Spirit fit into all this?

How do we nurture the presence of the Holy Spirit in this community?

The first one is fairly easy because of the examples already before us. In the bookstore things are so rigid, tied down, boxed in and controlled there is almost no way for the Holy Spirit to get a foothold anywhere. In the gym things are open, flexible, accessible-lots of openings. But, again, what's the difference? For that we take another look at Matthew's theory of authority. Remember, in that system of things, people are called (not ordered, delegated, directed) . . . called to some ministry or task. And they respond in faith and freedom. So, as a congregation, it seems to me our job is to assure that we are all free to respond, and that our faith is kept strong. If we are really good at that, we'll see so much authority bursting forth around here-well, it will be out of control!

November 16, 2003

TENTATIVELY

Thanksgiving Day Eve

It seems to me that Americans celebrate Thanksgiving Day . . . tentatively. Oh, it's not that we're not grateful (we are). And it's not that we don't have plenty to be thankful for (we do). It's just that, for me anyway, it's just that everything that I'm so grateful for, has an embarrassing flip-side to it.

I'm grateful for living in a free country with a democratic form of government. But what about those living under tyranny? Where it's not safe to speak your mind, think out loud or write or print your opinion? Where you dare not gather to openly discus matters of communal concern? Where you can't form labor unions, go on strike or vote? That's what I mean by the flip side.

I'm grateful for the rich companionship of a loving wife; for our caring and sharing and looking after one another. But what about those who must live alone and would rather not, or who live in constant fear of domestic violence?

I'm grateful for work that's satisfying and fulfilling, for nearly a whole lifetime of doing exactly what I feel most called to do and most blessed in doing; But what about those whose work is pure drudgery? Or who have no work?

I'm grateful for an abundance of food and for occasions to share a meal with family or friends. But what about those who will go to bed tonight (if they have a bed) hungry, and what about those who are starving while we feast?

I'm grateful for a comfortable home and clothes on my back; But what about those who are homeless or naked?

So, when I say "thanks" am I also claiming that I am somehow favored by God and singled out to be showered with God's blessings? No, I can't claim that; because I know that God has a passion for those who are almost my opposite; for the poor, the downtrodden, the lame, the blind, the widows and or-phans, the hungry, for refugees and prisoners, for the homeless and captives.

Part of the reason we are so well off in this country has nothing to do with God's blessings or with justice, but with our own fierce competitiveness and ambition, our corporate greed. We all know that, as a society, we are using up the world's resources and contributing to environmental pollution at rates way out of proportion to our numbers. I don't know that there is much any one of us can do about that; but we are all con-tributors!

So . . . We approach Thanksgiving . . . tentatively . . .

What then, makes Thanksgiving Day redeemable? Not just the day, but all occasions of being thankful, all ways of living thankfully?

"Remembering" is a key word here. If the "thanks" is to be real, it must carry with it a big element of remembering. If the thanks is genuine, it can't be a shallow, giddy, matter-of-fact utterance: it has to include a huge measure of remembering. Note that what makes the Great Thanksgiving great is not that we shout the thanks so loud, but that so much of it has to do with remembering. Most Eucharistic Prayers that I know of are predominantly about remembering.

We might, in fact, start out remembering God's mighty acts of creation: The vast expanse of interstellar space; stars, planets in their orbits, mountains, oceans, streams. We go on to recount salvation history; maybe starting with the call of Abraham and Sarah. Then there is the rescue of the children of Israel from Egypt, the crossing of the Red Sea, the wander-ing in the wilderness, the miracle of manna, water out of the rock. Then there is the recalling and reminding we receive in the words of the prophets: And so we remember and we give thanks together for that part of our heritage.

Finally we remember that on a certain night he gathered in

an upper room with his friends for their last meal together. He took bread, said the blessing, broke it and shared it declaring, "This is my body, eat it, and whenever you do this–remember me." Near the end of supper he took the cup of wine, blessed it, and passed it around saying, "This is my blood, it's a new covenant, and whenever you share the cup–remember me."

So, Thanksgiving Day is not about praising the Lord for all the stuff that surrounds us: It's about remembering who we are (The People of God), and remembering who God's children are (everybody). And with that I have a suggestion for you for this Thanksgiving Day. Tomorrow, when you are gathered around the table and someone has blessed the food you are about to share, have someone else take a roll or a slice of bread, break it and share it around the table, while all are invited to a moment of silence, and to . . . Remember.

BEING READY

Advent

The idea of Advent, as we are frequently reminded, is "be prepared," But it always seems to come across as such an impossible, and therefore discouraging, challenge: be alert, stay awake! However, the real challenge of Advent is, while demanding, still more encouraging and promising than usually perceived. Let's see if I can explain:

Many years ago, before the days of automobiles and motels, TV and even radio, The Lord decided to take a stroll around planet earth and see how things were faring with his people. Of course, if the Lord God wants to walk around in his creation just like an ordinary person, he can be any kind of person he chooses. So he decided to go as "Johnny," a run away teenager. That way, especially in those days, he'd draw very little attention to himself. He would go largely unnoticed.

The first day, as the sun was going down and Johnny was beginning to think about a place to lay over for the night, he approached two houses. On the left side of the road was a large, well-kept mansion with rolling lawns, big elm trees and a large stone wall–obviously the home of wealthy people. On the right side of the road was a small, humble but pleasant looking cottage, clearly the home of poor people. "Surely a kid would be no burden on a rich household for one night," mused the Lord. "I'll go there and not trouble these poor folk." So he went up to the big house, knocked on the door, and when the man came out, asked if there might be room for him to stay overnight. The man eyed the youngster up and down and said, "Well, maybe this looks like a large house –and indeed it is–but people of our means have many social obligations; we have no room for a drifter." He slammed the door.

So Johnny walked across the street to the little cottage and knocked. A man came to the door and once again the Lord made his request. "Why of course," said the man. "Travelers are sent from God; come on in and share what we have." The man's wife, who had heard the exchange from the kitchen, then approached. "Yes indeed, "she said, "I was just setting the table for supper. Come join us and I'll set another place." The three gathered around the table. She filled three bowls with steaming vegetable soup and placed a small loaf of freshly baked bread on the table. The man then asked God's blessing on the food, on themselves and on the poor, the homeless and the hungry everywhere. They then sat down, broke the bread and shared the meal.

After supper the woman made ready the only bed they had and invited their new friend, Johnny to take his rest, explaining that she and her husband often slept on the porch where there was a nice breeze. The Lord at first objected to the arrangement, but when they insisted that it really was no hardship, he turned in and was soon fast asleep.

The next morning he awakened to busy sounds in the kitchen and the wonderful aroma of breakfast underway. Once more he joined the couple for a simple but good meal, and prepared to take his leave. However, he was so touched by the graciousness of these good people that he paused, thought for a moment and decided to leave them with a special blessing. He first revealed who he really was; then proceeded to offer them his blessing in the form of three wishes fulfilled. Well, the couple hardly knew what to make of that. They liked this kid and wanted to be his friend, but God? Of course the Lord understood their problem, so he urged them to try the wishes.

The man looked at his wife, then back to the Lord. "Well", he said for both of them, "we have just about everything we need; what is there to wish for?"

"Go ahead, you'll think of something." They looked at each other again, and this time the woman spoke. "We hope for eternal life," she said. "I suppose you could call that a wish?"

"You've got it," said the Lord. "how about another?"

The woman spoke again–kind of catching on to the procedure. Í wish for good health and daily bread for the rest of our time here on earth."

"Granted," said the Lord. "But you still have one wish more."

Again the couple looked at each other, then at the youth, "We can't think of anything we need." (Actually, the Lord wanted to impress them, so they would indeed know that he was the Lord). How about a new house?" he offered. "Wouldn't you like to have a nice big house like the people across the street?"

They checked each other once more. "Well, yes, that would be nice," they agreed. And while they stood there, the house around them was transformed into a beautiful mansion. This done, the Lord bid them farewell and trudged on down the road.

Sometime later the man across the way awakened. He stood up, stretched, threw open the drapes and was astounded to see, across the street, a house every bit as fine as his. He called his wife. They both stood there gawking, hardly believing their eyes. She rubbed the window pane. It was no illusion. He quickly dressed, ran over to the new house and inquired of the owner how they had managed to pull that off. They, of course, explained the whole encounter of the night before, when a homeless lad appeared at the door, supper together, then the morning and the three wishes. "Why," said the rich man, "he came to our house first; the three wishes were meant for us!" "Well, we don't know about that," said the poor man, who was having enough trouble getting accustomed to these new surroundings. And the rich man went back to his humble (all is relative) surroundings.

He explained to his wife: "They told me that he left, walking west; maybe I can catch him." He saddled one of his finest horses, hopped on and went galloping west on the old dirt road. About two hours later he caught up with the teenager, whom he now believed just might be God. They stood at the side of the road; the horse, lathered, was glad for the break and chance to catch his breath. The rich man explained, "But I didn't know you were God." The Lord patiently heard him out as he enumerated his excuses and explained the extenuating circumstances, finally ending up with a case for why he should also receive three wishes.

The Lord explained that his grace was on all his people, but three wishes–well that was extraordinary, not for everyone. "I'm afraid you wouldn't know what to do with three wishes," he said. In fact, I'm quite sure they would not work well for you."

But the rich man persisted, reminding God that he was a for-giving God, until the Lord finally said, "All right, have it your way. You have three wishes." With that the youth turned and contin-ued westward on the dusty road.

The rich man, elated, mounted his somewhat rested steed and galloped off to the east to share the good news with his wife. After about an hour of hard riding, as they rounded a bend in the road, the horse stumbled and nearly went down. The impatient rider cursed the animal: "You stupid beast; I wish you'd break your neck," whereupon the poor animal immediately dropped dead. A couple of hours later the man was trudging up the road, toting the heavy saddle, the sun beating down on him, when he went over a little rise and could see his house far off in the distance. "Oh, how I wish I had a large cup of cold water." On the side of the road, he spied a spring and a tin cup hanging from a twig nearby. "How lucky," he thought, as he quenched his thirst. Then it occurred to him that he had already used up two of his three wishes, and he wasn't even home yet.

A couple of hours later the tired adventurer got home and relayed all to his wife. Only one wish left. What would it be? They paced back and forth. Every so often they glanced out the front window at the mansion across the street, and every time they did they got angrier. Finally the Mrs. exploded. "Why we've always had the big house on this street. Now theirs is just as big. I wish we had a palace five times the size of theirs." And while they stood there, the mansion around them was transformed into a beautiful palace.

Several years later–it was still before the days of automo-biles and motels, TV and even radio–God decided to take a stroll around planet earth and see how things were faring with her people. Of course if God wants to walk around in her creation, she can be any kind of person she chooses. So, she decided to go as "Marie", a milkmaid. That way, especially in those days, she'd draw very little attention to herself. She would go largely unno-ticed.

The first day as the sun was going down and Marie was begin-ning to think about a place to lay over for the night, she ap-proached two mansions.

The house on the left was, in fact, huge. The one on the right looked especially friendly, with shade trees and large flower and vegetable gardens. "Well," she thought, recalling an earlier encounter in this neighborhood, "Guess I'll look in on the rich folk." She rattled the door knocker and waited. Soon a pompous looking man in starched shirt and velvet jacket appeared. She could hear music and laughter in the background; clearly there was a big party underway. The little milkmaid explained that she was traveling and needed a place to sleep, and maybe something to eat. He looked her up and down and answered, "I'm sure this looks like the home of people of means, and so it is, but we are also people of considerable social responsibility. We have no room for the likes of you!" And he slammed the door

So Marie went across the street and knocked on that door. The woman of the house answered, and the same question was put. "Certainly," she said, "come on in; always room for one more. We were just getting ready for supper; I'll set another place." They proceeded into the large dining room. The banquet-size table must have had twenty or more settings. About that time young people started coming in through several doors. The woman's husband explained, "You see, we are not really wealthy people, but . . . several years ago . . . well, it's a complicated story; let's just say a miracle occurred and we found ourselves in this lovely house where there was once a modest cottage. Anyway, we felt so blessed in having a place like this, we simply had to share it. So we've made it into a home for runaway teens. They come here, stay with us for a while until they get their bearings; help with the chores and garden, then move on. And now we are twice blessed: for the home, of course, but now also for the love that fills it."

The whole household gathered around the table. This time it was one of the kids who asked God's blessing; on the food, on all present, on the poor, the homeless and the hungry everywhere. The food seemed especially delicious that evening.

After supper those on duty quickly cleared the table, washed the dishes, and set up for breakfast next day. Then, as was their custom, they gathered around a large fireplace for evening re-laxation and talk. Everybody was curious about their new friend, the little milkmaid, and she held their rapt attention. She spoke of life and adventure in far off places and among strange people and customs. She talked of love and dignity, about vocation, service and fulfillment. She seemed to know all about the animals of the world, about growing things from oak trees to moss, and she treated all God's creation with such reverence and awe that her listeners felt chills run up their spines and their hair stand on end. Everyone in the room knew that they were very special and incredibly important people.

The next morning, after breakfast, and with hugs all around, Marie departed, heading west down the dusty road. For a long time husband and wife stood at the door, hand in hand, while suspicious eyes peered at them from a window across the street. Finally the young stranger rounded a bend in the road and disappeared. The woman turned to her husband: "Did not our hearts burn within us, while she spoke to us last night by the fire?" They turned back to the door-and a thrice blessed household.

So the idea of Advent is not to be prepared in the sense that we must gird up our loins, be eternally vigilant, disciplined, alert, always awake and ready -- even frightened and anxious. That's an impossible demand. No, the idea of Advent is that we be so immersed in the Grace of God that we are, just naturally, ready.

December 14, 2003

ROOM AT THE INN

Christmas Eve

"Because there was no room at the Inn . . ." No place for them in the inn! Luke doesn't bother to explain, but it kind of makes the innkeeper sound like a weasel, doesn't it? In all the traveling I've done, I've sure stayed at a lot of inns. I usually go for a Holiday Inn. It isn't exactly "top drawer," but, like McDonald's, there is usually one there, and it's predictable -- no surprises -- you know what to expect. I've stayed at a lot of other places too. Sometimes with cockroaches, one time with bed-bugs, several times with lizards running all over the place; one sang to me all night. And there have been a few times, in raunchy surroundings, where the door latch didn't work because it had been broken into so many times. It's not easy to get a good night's sleep in those kinds of hotels. I've been hustled out of my room twice in the middle of the night because of fire alarms, and once awoke to screams in the next room where a burglar had broken in. So, I value predictability in choosing an inn.

I'm thinking right now however, of a particular trip. It was a long time ago, and I was living in the east in those days, and it was Christmas. I was working out of the Diocese of Bethlehem in eastern Pennsylvania, and, at the time, I had a contract with an Appalachian church group serving the whole Appalachian range from Atlanta to Albany. The diocese was part of this coalition of dioceses. The group was known as APSO and I was a consultant to APSO. The trip was down to some little town in east Tennessee, to attend a conference on Appalachian poverty, and it was scheduled the week before Christmas. I was going because I represented APSO's interests.

There was also a young woman of Trinity Parish, Bethlehem, who was going to represent the Diocese of Bethlehem. We would be traveling together. I had some misgivings about this, for she was about nine months pregnant. However, she was strong, self assured, and she had a passion for poor people. She was involved in many parish and community programs dealing with local poverty, and she wasn't about to miss this regional meeting. So we made our flight plans, but I was unable to get lodging for us at the local Holiday Inn. There was no local Holiday Inn. However, we did get there, and the local folk provided the accommodations–frugal, but adequate. The conference came off as planned. Then it was time to go home.

Almost! As it turned out, we had a little extra time and she had some last minute Christmas shopping to do. There was a mall nearby, so the two of us made our way to the mall.

What a zoo! I don't care much for malls anyway, but this was ridiculous. The place was jammed, total chaos, bell ringers at every door. A Salvation Army band was out of tune and competing with the sacred music on the loudspeakers: "Rudolph the Red Nosed Reindeer" and "Jingle Bells." Last minute sales pitches ran rampant: "Prices slashed!" Buy two, get both!" "Don't worry about the payments–we'll get them!" Into this cacophony of chaos and confusion came two lonely figures.

Now, I should mention that when you go to an Appalachian conference on poverty, you don't dress up in your finery. You wear your grungies; it adds to the atmosphere. So there I was in an old pair of western boots, thread-bare Levis, and rough coat; she as plainly dressed and great with child, like a couple of people just in from the hills; confusion, noise, and crowding all around.

She picked out some stuff and we made our way through the line to the cash register. As soon as we opened our mouths the sales clerk knew we were Yankees. "Oh y'all are visitin' here, aren't you? Where y'all from?"

"Bethlehem" we responded in unison. She paused, quizzical look on her face, as she stole another, more careful look at my companion. Then, "How kin I hep ya?"

We walked away chuckling quietly. It happened twice more that evening. Finally it was time to get on out to the airport. We went outside. It was dark, lightly snowing. We hailed a cab. The cabbie was very considerate, helping her slide sideways onto the seat. At the airport he once again assisted her, southern gentleman that he was. Then, "Where y'all headed for t'night?" "Bethlehem," we said. He checked her out once more, then without another word, walked around the cab to the driver's side. We got home a little later that night and a few days after Christmas, she delivered a baby boy.

"Because there was no room for them at the inn." Let's come back to that line. As I said, Luke doesn't bother to explain. But I have access to some other sources, and I'd like to tell you just what did happen that night.

First, we have to remember that there were no Holiday Inns in first century Palestine. There wasn't even anything like a Holiday Inn. An inn in first century Palestine was more like a courtyard. It was a place to gain some protection from highway bandits overnight. There were no sheets, no little bars of soap, no showers–no accommodations at all, except the wall and the gate. So travelers arrived with their families and animals and, for a price, were permitted room at the "inn." Then they had to fend for themselves: Find a quiet corner perhaps, tether the animals, arrange bedding for the kids and hope for the best. No privacy, no guarantees, except that the gate would be locked.

On this particular night the people had gathered from all over for the census. The town was crowded and the inn was packed. And "there was no place for them in the inn." Of course an innkeeper in that kind of setting can always find room for a couple more. But let's take in the picture. Here are a dozen men over on this side with a couple of skins of wine, singing songs, telling old stories and having a grand old time–it's a family reunion. Then, over there, a group of teens, probably cousins, with a variety of musical instruments, all out of tune. Then this tipsy guy leads his camel down the center, crowding through, and the camel stomps all over this woman's sack of dates. Over in that corner a family with six kids is trying to get bedded down, but the youngest has a toothache and screams all night. In that other corner, over there a little fellow with a full beard jumps up to confront the big guy, "Hey, you, did you see what your donkey did on my bedroll?" Meantime, shysters and opportunists roam about hawking their wares. It's noisy, loud, confusing, utter chaos! The only thing I can think of in 21st century America to compare with it would be a shopping mall two nights before Christmas.

Now, with all this racket, bustle and confusion, there comes a rattle at the gate. The old innkeeper goes to the gate, opens it, and steps outside to confront two frightened teenagers. One is a ragged, worn, tired young man. The other, a pregnant girl who looks like she probably won't make it down another city block. He eyes the woman up and down, then turns to the guy. "Hey, man, this ain't no place for her!" He scratches his head, thinking. Then, "Come with me."

He leads them down a path, off at an angle and down the hill. A little way, then the path switches back, still going downhill, along the face of a cliff, under the inn. The noise of the inn fades. They come to a gate. The old man opens it. "This is my corral, where I keep my donkey and a couple of goats. Hardly anybody knows about this place. You'll be safe here."

They continue along the face of the cliff. All is quiet now. The noise from the inn doesn't get down here. They come to a cave. "This is the shelter for my animals," he says. "It's clean and dry, and there's plenty of straw for bedding; you should be comfortable." They go into the wide-mouthed cave. "See," the old man says, "it's not even dark." They look. The cave opens to the western sky and the bright stars dispel the darkness of the cave. The old innkeeper turns and trudges back up the path. He disappears from sight, and soon they hear the gate open-and close again. In the stillness of the night, two youngsters arrange the straw, and fall asleep with a million stars dancing in the sky just outside the cave. Later that night they are awakened by the sound of the angels singing. It was time!

And, of course, that's why we are here tonight, isn't it? Like the old innkeeper, to get away from the clatter, racket and chaos of our lives for a spell and find a quiet place in our hearts for the holy family . . . and perhaps, hear the angels sing. It's that time!

CONTRACT WITH GOD

Baptismal Covenant I

We all know what a contract is -- say a twenty-year mortgage on the house or a five-year, new car loan. On the one hand (my end of the deal) I agree to make the monthly payments for the period specified. On the other hand, the lender agrees to let me use his money for a while so I can afford to get something I want. My monthly payments include interest. So, the interest is what the lender gets out of the deal.

The same kind of thing happens when I go into a hardware store to get a screwdriver. I select the screwdriver I want. The price is acceptable. So we make the exchange. I get the screwdriver, the merchant gets the money. We have negotiated and executed a contract on the spot.

Now, in all these transactions it is assumed that the parties to the contract are basically equal. We live under the same law of the land; we are familiar with the same social norms and procedures; we have equal rights and so on. A covenant however, is a special kind of contract. A covenant is an agreement between unequal parties. In a covenant the superior party can offer the agreement to an inferior party. The inferior party can accept or not, but the inferior party can not initiate. Here we are dealing with a covenant.

Our Baptismal covenant is in two parts. The first part is, basically, the Apostles Creed. It is ontological-having to do with who we are. The questions ask "Do you believe . . .?" And the responses, essentially are, "I do," The second part is existential. It has to do with promised actions with questions such as, "Will you . . . ? And responses; "I will with God's help." This is the part I will take up today. There are five queries. And remember, the sense of it is that God is offering us the opportunity of living in this covenant. God is not forcing us, we do have a choice. But in

God's grace we have the offer before us.

Will you continue in the apostles' teaching and fellowship, in the breaking of bread, and in the prayers?

In the second chapter of the book of Acts we have Luke's account of Pentecost. It's a message of ecstasy and confusion as the Spirit is poured into the brand new church, and the people start babbling in tongues and conveying the general impression of being drunk. Peter takes charge, standing before the crowd, preaching the Good News. And he really gets charged up, for, we are told, they added to their numbers that day about three thousand souls. Then, Luke writes: "They devoted themselves to the apostles' teaching and fellowship, to the breaking of bread and the prayers." That quote from Acts has become one of the classic, brief descriptions of the essential nature of the church, so we find it embodied in the first promise of our covenant.

Notice that we promise to continue. We are already on the journey; our promise is to stay the course in the apostles' teaching (sound doctrine-good theology) . . . and fellowship (remain in the community). Notice how the parts are interdependent. We can't do one of them alone. That's why church attendance is so important. It keeps us on track on both counts; continuous exposure to the scripture and the continuing company of other members of the faith community. And that is part and parcel of the last two promises-to continue in the breaking of bread (Eucharistic fellowship) and the prayers-both personal and corporate.

Will you persevere in resisting evil, and, whenever you fall into sin, repent and return to the Lord?

We have already covered the sense of these promises earlier in the service of Holy Baptism in the Examination of the Candidates (see page 302, BCP) where we renounced all things evil or sinful. Now here, as if to underline the importance of these matters, we promise to "persevere in resisting evil." It's a never ending process. The phrase I want to call your attention to is one that is easily overlooked: whenever you fall into sin. Not if you fall into sin, but whenever. Falling into sin is falling away from God, and it is assumed that we will. But that's not the last word. When that happens -- when you catch yourself in that place -- repent (turn around-about face) and return to the Lord.

Will you proclaim by word and example the Good News of God in Christ?

I honestly believe that there is a lot more of this going on than most people think. Given my years as a theologian and a pastor, I suspect that I am more in tune with this than the average person. I simply see it all over the place. And most Christians I observe "proclaiming by word and example" are doing it naturally. They are not particularly conscious of witnessing to their baptismal covenant, and that's the way it should be.

I think for example, of a group of high school kids that I knew a few years back at Intercession Parish, Thornton, CO. They had a regular Sunday morning class and they had their regular teacher, but I filled in on occasion. One morning (we were talking about the Ten Commandments) they started discussing experiences in public school, in social studies, on the subject of capital punishment. Most of their classmates (I gather) strongly supported the death penalty. One youngster reported an incident in his class. They had been considering a trial in progress in Denver where the death penalty was at stake. The pro-death members of the class (in the public school) dominated the discussion, not only with their hard attitudes but with their emotion-laden arguments. The kids in my (church school) class were shocked at the report, making remarks such as "Oooooo, that's sick!" I was very proud of them. They were not conscious of "proclaiming by word and example", but I was aware of what was going on.

Will you seek and serve Christ in all persons, loving your neighbor as yourself?

I believe it was Will Rogers who said, "I never met a man I didn't like." I can go along with that just fine, but the key is the word "met." If we have truly met the other person, we know his idiosyncrasies (which give him character), her flaws (which we can overlook), her finer qualities (about which we have mixed feelings). And the better we know the individual, the more acceptable, the more understandable the more loveable the person. When we really know the other person, it's nearly impossible not to like her. The problem is we seldom get to know people that well.

The second part of this one is probably more of a problem (for most of us) than the first. The implication that I'm supposed to love myself doesn't seem modest enough. We live in a culture where one is expected to put oneself down, make excuses for one's talents, disown one's achievements; never mind honesty, modesty is the rule. But self acceptance is much healthier. Narcissus' problem was not self love but the love of his image. That's a different matter. Here we promise to love our neighbor as ourselves. Or we can turn that around for a little different perspective, "love yourself the same as you love your neighbor." Maybe that gets at it a little better; the point is to discover Christ in everyone around us including ourselves.

Will you strive for justice and peace among all people, and respect the dignity of every human being?

In our striving for justice and peace it is necessary sometimes that we hold some very unsavory characters to account. In extreme cases, we might even find it necessary to confine persistent offenders for the protection of the general public. Rehabilitation is always the preferred course. (People ought always have the option to "repent and return to the Lord.") But, it appears that, for whatever reason, there are those who can't or won't. So it is that, in society's striving for justice and peace among all people, we must, on occasion, take someone out of circulation for life. We do what we have to do. But we never do it out of revenge. The second part of our vow takes revenge out of the equation. We respect the dignity of every human being always, everywhere, under all circumstances. The terrible sin at Abu Ghraib was no show of respect for anybody's dignity; a massive violation of the dignity of prisoners under our command. But, under such circumstances everybody's dignity is trashed. In the photos we saw of prisoners and guards there was no dignity anywhere.

So there, briefly is the substance of our contract with God; our Baptismal Covenant. The theme "covenant" runs throughout Hebrew and Christian scriptures. God made a covenant with Adam, with Noah, with Moses to mention just a few examples. In fact, another word for "covenant" is "testament." Thus the whole of our collection of Hebrew Scriptures is about covenant (The Old Testament) and the whole of our collection of Christian Scriptures is about covenant (The New Testament). In a few places in scripture covenant is dealt with explicitly. It forms the backdrop, however, for the whole Bible. If we were to take, say, a year to study the theme "Covenant" in the Bible, we would in effect be studying the history of God's offerings of grace and blessings to God's creation. God's offering is before us today.

RESURRECTION

Easter 2004

When Lynne and I were married (way back in 1982) I had never met any of her family. We had met in Alaska where she was on the diocesan staff. I was in private practice as a management consultant working out of New Jersey and with a contract with the Diocese of Alaska. Lynne later took a position with the Diocese of Olympia and moved to Seattle. Over the years, we were in touch with some regularity since we both were involved with a number of professional networks. We were married in Arizona and established Colorado as our base of operations. Her parents and her only sibling and his family all lived in the hill country of Texas. So, shortly after the wedding we decided that we should haul ourselves down to Kerrville, Texas and give her family a chance to check out this new member of their clan. All went very well. I fell in love with three little kids and Lynne's parents apparently concluded that Lynne was OK for the time being.

During our stay in Kerrville, Lynne's mother brought out two albums she had been assembling. One was a photo history of Lynne, from her baby pictures, through her years in school, right up to her time in Alaska where I had met her. A similar collection was a history of her brother. Well, I just claimed the Lynne collection; didn't ask for it, just kept it, and nobody objected. I've treasured the album ever since. Even today I can browse through that album and see a pair of dimples set just a tad lower than dimples usually appear; there's always a smile that ever so slightly turns down at the corners of her mouth. I recognize a characteristic gesture or a familiar mannerism. Oh, it's Lynne all right. And gradually I've come to realize that the woman I love so much today is not just the person I'm living with today; it's the person represented by that collection of photos, plus over twenty years on a shared journey. Love transcends time, embraces all time, has no time boundaries. It's like I'm in love with the total Lynne; the timeless Lynne.

So, today we celebrate the day of the resurrection. Of course scripture clearly witnesses to the resurrection of Jesus the Christ. But scripture also asserts that we are included in Christ's res- urrection–we, members of the Body of Christ, share in Christ's resurrection. But what does that mean? How do we take that? Literally, spiritually, figuratively?

I remember, back in the late sixties, my middle daughter was in high school; and she was a child of her time: (a) she was a hippy, carried all her belongings, including a guitar, around in a guitar case. She would not shave under her arms or wear a bra. (b) She was also a "Jesus freak." Those were young people who loved Jesus, read the Bible but never went to church. One of her friends asked her very seriously one time, "Is your father for real?" Meaning, I guess, does he really believe like we do? And (c) she was (still is) a serious environmentalist. It was about this time she came to me with a question about the resurrection. "Dad, do you believe in life after death?"

Well, how do you deal with such a question in a few words, especially with a fifteen-year-old? I gave it some hasty thought and decided to respond to the environmentalist. "Honey" I said, "You already know how the Lord recycles everything: leaves that fall from the trees become soil in which other trees can take root." and so on and so on. She already appreciated that. "Well" I continued, "some of the most precious things in life–gifts from God–are things like relationships, affection, character, intel- ligence, personhood, even personality; it seems to me that the God I know must have a way to preserve or recycle all that -- the most precious stuff of creation -- as well as leaves and grass." I never did figure out if that reached her.

Paul apparently had to deal with such questions from the church in Corinth. This is from his first letter to the Corinthians: But, someone will ask, "How are the dead raised? With what kind of body do they come?" Paul responds to his rhetorical ques- tion with a series of metaphors mostly having to do with planting seeds. Hear the contrasts in this series, What is sown is perish- able, what is raised is imperishable; it is sown in dishonor, it is raised in glory; it is sown in weakness, it is raised in power. It is sown a physical body; it is raised a spiritual body. Notice the element of continuity. If you plant a petunia seed, you'll soon see a petunia blossoming; you won't get a radish. The identity of the thing remains. But notice also the discontinuity. The petunia is no longer a seed, it's a blossom. Paul sums up this transformation, It is sown a physical body, it is raised a spiritual body. I suppose another way of saying it would be It is sown an earthly creation, it is raised a heavenly being. But how are we to understand this "spiritual body" or this "heavenly being?" How can we-here and now-get some sense of what this means?

Well, let's create a context in which we might be able to "see" this. Theologically, we have known since the time of Augustine that, counter-intuitively, time and space are not endless continuities in which God created suns, planets, moons and everything else. Time and space are part of what God created. Time and space had a beginning and will have an end. And we have known the scientific truth of this since Einstein proved it in the last century.

In fact, for Einstein and colleagues, "time-space" is a single reality, but certainly part of the created order. On another occasion I've discussed with you the two Greek words for time. The Greek chronos is clock time; day follows day, season follows season. Time is circular, like going around on a merry-go-round. In this view of things, time has little or no meaning-it just goes round and round. Then there is kairos-THE time-the point when eternity slams into chronos and fills it with meaning.

For the history of humanity the great kairos of all time was the Christ event. In the incarnation eternity crashed into history. Henceforth all time before the incarnation must be understood as leading to-preparing for-the Christ event. And all history following the incarnation is seen as working out the significance of the Christ event. The symbol for this is: "The Kingdom of God." For individuals, kairos can break into our time line in many ways, yet it is always the same. Actually the common English translation of kairos, "in the fullness of time" is a good description of our experience of kairos; a time when time itself seems filled to the brim; exploding with meaning. So, we live our lives day by day, year by year, but God transcends our experience of time except when kairos bursts in upon us, and we get a taste of eternity.

Many years ago I was flying into Kelowna, British Columbia for a consultation. Kelowna is on the Okinagan, a huge, very deep lake, home of Ogopogo, a lake critter something like the Loc Ness monster. Our entry into Kelowna took us south following the western shore of the lake. It was winter. I looked down and could see a freight train winding it's way south on a track following the shore. Of course, from my vantage point I could see the track miles ahead of the train and miles behind it. The train crew couldn't see beyond the next curve. The crew didn't know it yet, but they were about to experience a BIG delay in their plans. What I could see that they could not, was a big snow drift across the track directly ahead of them.

Now if I might use that space image as a metaphor for time: Think of our experience of time as something like the train crew's experience of the track. We experience time mostly as a series of events or happenings gradually unfolding before us with the future basically unknown. But God sees our whole time frame at a glance–past, present, future–as I could see the whole track at once. That doesn't mean that God manipulates or controls. But from the perspective of eternity, all of chronos is experienced in an instant.

Back to Paul's rhetorical question: How are the dead raised? With what kind of body do they come? And his metaphorical response, It is sown a physical body; it is raised a spiritual body. He further describes it as imperishable, in glory, in power. But let me personalize the question to make it a little more tangible. When my time is up, what will the Lord save of me? Will it be the me that is in this point in chronos? Old, weak, worn out, tired? No, I don't think so. God has a lot more to work with than the empty shell that remains. I think that what God will recycle as my spiritual body will be, for example, the curious, wide-eyed youngster full of wonder that was me over seventy years ago. It'll be the kid on a summer day lying in the grass watching the variety of cloud formations changing and drifting across the sky. It'll be the rapidly maturing adolescent beginning to discover the full richness of life and love and passion. It'll have a fair portion of the idealism of a seventeen year old volunteering for a tour of duty. There will be a good measure of the young lover eager for the experience of fatherhood. The ideals, principles and faith that have been guiding me will continue to define who I am; the relationships that have sustained me, the wisdom that has nurtured me and given growth year by year will be raised with me. "A pretty big order," you might say. Well, let me put it this way: If I, mere mortal, can love another human being in a way that absolutely transcends time–a kairos sort of way; surely God can!

DECALOGUE

Orders From on High ... or Revelation?

As we continue our journeys in faith we need to continually challenge our grasp of the theological basics such as the Creed, the Ten Commandments, the Baptismal Covenant and so on. Lent is a good time to take that up, and considering our current practice of reciting the Decalogue each week as part of our Sunday liturgy, it suggests that a review of the law might be timely.

I'll start off with a question: Should we consider the Decalogue a revelation concerning God's design for humanity or is it a list of regulations we are expected to live up to? The way they are formulated and the way people generally talk about them, it seems clear: this is the LAW plain and simple. However, I think I can show you that it can't work that way. If we try to accept the Decalogue as a list of rules we are supposed to try real hard to obey, we'll get nowhere with them. Try to experience the Decalogue as the gracious gift of a loving God. God is not saying "You shall," and "You shall not," It's more like: "Here's the pattern of human living I intended." Try to think of it that way as we proceed.

Then there is a second point I'd like to make up front. Remember that the Decalogue originally came to us in the Hebrew language. The form that we have before us is, of course an English translation. Still, some of the peculiarities of the Hebrew come through in the English. Hebrew is a very poetic language; it is not one for highly abstract thinking or generalizing. Hebrew is concrete, specific; it is the language of the prophets. Greek is the language of the philosophers. An example: The tenth commandment is: You shall not covet. However in the Hebrew original it goes on to list all the things you must not covet; Your neighbor's wife, your neighbor's field, his ox, his donkey and on and on. One might be inclined to think that coveting my neighbor's Buick is alright, since that's not on the list. (There is a catch-all in the list however; "or anything that is your neighbor's.")

Paul, on the other hand, (writing in the Greek) quotes this commandment simply as, "You shall not covet."(Romans 7:7) The objects are all dropped off. The point of the commandment, Paul seems to be saying, is not the object of my coveting, but the big ego, the big "I" that is doing the coveting. Considered this way, the real offense here is self-centeredness. And the root of self-centeredness is self-consciousness, which is a product of our experience in the Garden of Eden. According to that story, you will recall, the woman, tempted by the serpent, ate the forbidden fruit of the tree of the knowledge of good and evil, shared it with her husband and the two became as gods, knowing good and evil. They knew they were naked, and tried to hide from God; the beginning of self-consciousness. Let's go on then and take these commandments up one by one. However I'm going to adjust the order some. (Moses, I think, got them mixed up.)

(1) You shall have no other gods but me. Of course, there are no other gods. So what's the point? At the time of the Hebrew migration out of Egypt (when Moses received the revelation of the Decalogue), there were all kinds of "other gods." The point is that for the Jewish people there were to be no other gods. They were to be faithful and zealous followers of the one God who called them and sent them to be a priestly people to the nations. This kind of faith is called henothism. There may be many gods, but we are called to be faithful followers of one in particular. A little theological reflection on the point makes it clear that there can be only one god. I can define god as my, "highest point of reference." If I then go on to call "A" God and "B" Satan, (which would be akin to claiming good and evil gods) I am clearly using something else as a higher point of reference from which I can make such judgments about what is "good" and what is "evil." This higher point of reference is then my "god."

(10) You shall not covet. As we have seen above, the problem here is self- centeredness; the big "I" doing the desiring. Paul Tillich explains it this way: Our ancestors in the Garden of Eden (pre-self conscious creatures) were in a state of innocence. When they succumbed to temptation their eyes were opened and they knew good from evil; they were subject to guilt. Tillich's anal-

ogy is a sexual relationship. When a couple find themselves attracted to one another they are faced with a kind of Garden of Eden dilemma. They are, initially, innocent. However temptation is right there. If they succumb to temptation and enter into sexual union, innocence (at least as far as that relationship is concerned) is gone forever. If, however, they resist temptation, the potential and the promise of a fulfilling sexual union are forfeited. The potential is unrealized and fulfillment incomplete. That was the dilemma of Eve in the garden.

She succumbed and humanity lives with the consequences. We are now self-conscious beings, fully aware of our sin and guilt. Thank God for Eve! We cannot go back to that state of innocence of our mythical ancestors in the garden (Who wants to?) we can only go forward, accept our guilt and move ahead in God's grace. Which brings us back to our earlier point: We can't take the Decalogue as a list of rules we must try real hard to obey. If we desire to comply with the 10 commandments, we've blown it because we have already violated number ten. You shall not covet. There is no getting around it; the "commandments" cannot be taken as law, they can only be seen as a revelation of God, and our salvation is by God's grace not by obedience to some set of rules.

In trying to explain this to a group of youngsters years ago, one lad responded, "But, Father Wilson, I can't help it; when my friend gets a new model plane, I do covet it!" So we discussed it some more. Eventually I saw his eyes light up and he stood up to explain, "I see what you mean, You mean that if I love my friend enough, then when he gets something new, I'll feel good for him, and then I'll be obeying the commandment without even thinking about it."

"You got it," I said. Still, how do we get ourselves to that place where the commandments reflect our actual human nature? Or, as Jeremiah describes this ideal situation, "I will put my law within them, and I will write it upon their hearts." (Jer. 31: 33) In other words, what is needed here is that we be the kind of people the Decalogue sets forth, not that we get ourselves into a constant fight within ourselves trying to act in harmony with the law. Paul puts it this way: "The Gentiles who did not pursue righteousness attained it, that is, righteousness through faith; Israel who pursued righteousness which is based on law did not succeed in fulfilling that law. Why? Because they did not pursue it through faith, but as if it were based on works." What we count on here is God's grace not our super will, or good works.

(2 and 7) You shall not make for yourself any idol. You shall not commit adultery.   I'll treat these two as one. Moses separated them, I suppose, because he was thinking in terms of Hebrew, which doesn't do well with abstract thinking. And, granted, number two (idols) does follow well on the heels of number one, (no other gods). If I am fully reconciled to the idea of one god, I'm stuck; no out. God is God and I am creature, No wiggle room. However, Me being Me, I'll look for some wiggle room anyway. (This argument is continuous with that on number ten [coveting] It's the big "I" that's the problem).

So, no other gods! Well maybe I can reduce god down to something a little more manageable. Then, I'm still in charge. I'll turn god into a thing I can handle, manipulate, use for my purposes. Isaiah pokes fun at this kind of religion; "when your enemy threatens, you have to run off with your gods, to save them. What kind of god is that?"

Anyway, the basic problem is turning God into an object that I can use for my ends. It's entirely backwards. It's God's agenda that's supposed to be guiding things and it's my responsibility to bring myself into line with that. If I don't, then I am in rebellion, (sin) and that won't work, except for my destruction. This was the problem with the pagan religions surrounding Israel. Gods were associated with the growing cycle, fertility in the flock and all those seasonal contingencies associated with agriculture. Religion had to do with appeasing the gods in order to assure that there would be sufficient seasonal rain, that each ewe would bear twins and so on. In other words the pagan people were pursuing their agenda and the challenge was one of manipulating the fates, forces of nature or "gods" to their ends.

The revelation that came to the children of Israel, of course, turned this completely upside down. God was in charge; it was God's agenda; there was no manipulating; living in harmony with God's creation the way God created it was the only way to go. It is hard for us to imagine the total revolution -- reversals -- in human thinking this represented. However, it isn't so difficult for us to see the problem in pagan manifestations of it; reducing god to the status of a thing that can be used. There are plenty of idols in our lives. Think of all the forces that unduly influence our day-to-day decisions; pride of ownership for example (a new car, house, boat or whatever.) Or consider what's at stake; my reputation for starters; (gotta be able to hold my head up). Oh, there are plenty of forces out there besides love driving our lives. We are not free of idolatry.

Adultery is a closely related problem. It has been pointed out that the first four commandments have to do with our relationships with God; the last six, with our relationships with one another. Idolatry (number 2) is to the first set as adultery (number 7) is to the second set. Adultery, taking it literally (as in the Hebrew) is infidelity in marriage; or, even more specifically, infidelity of a woman in marriage. (Have you ever heard the story of the man taken in adultery -- in the very act?) But we are abstracting from the Hebrew to better understand this stuff in terms of our own time and culture. So considered, I'm going to ask you to think of adultery as reducing another human being to the status of a thing, an object, that one can then use for one's own purposes. Now you can probably see the connection between these two commandments. And, I think when you see the connection, you'll have a greater appreciation of the depth and seriousness of each, since each sheds light on the other.

Using another person for my own gratification is what we are considering here. Using is a key term. Things are intended for using. People are for relationships. "Use things; love people," as the old cliché goes. Oh, how easy to get that reversed. Love things; use people. We need only think of the low status of the prostitute in society, the lowest of the low. The way all this goes over in common street talk is revealing of the deep personal offence involved. It hinges on the "f" word. ("F….. you"; "Boy did I get f----d in that transaction!") and its countless variations. The point is, a deeply ingrained cultural offense exists in the act we call adultery—using another person for our own sexual gratification. It is so deep and so pervasive it can almost go unnoticed. We tend to become insensitive to it.

Backing off from a literal understanding of adultery, we can appreciate the point of this in a broader context. Adultery, so considered, isn't only infidelity in marriage, but in any relationship. If the interpersonal love and mutual respect people have come to count on in any situation is violated by someone using another as an object or a thing for one's own gratification or profit, we are right on the turf of this commandment. This changes the boundaries. It no longer depends entirely on whether or not a marriage is involved. Fidelity might characterize any relationship, and a married couple might be found using each other for purely selfish ends.

So, idolatry-adultery; much the same thing. The big problem here as we've seen, is the big "I" that keeps getting in the way. It presses one to take charge in one's relations with God and it drives one to master one's relationships with others. It just can't work that way. "Wretched man that I am! Who will deliver me from this body of death? Thanks be to God through Jesus Christ our Lord." (Romans 7: 24-25)

(3)You shall not take the Lord's name in vain. The basic idea here is to not attribute to the Lord something that is contrary to the Lord's purpose or character. You'll recall the story of Balaam's donkey. (Numbers 22) Balak, king of Moab, wanted Balaam, the prophet to curse the children of Israel so they couldn't overrun the land. However Balaam knew that the children of Israel (fresh out of Egypt, on their trek to the Promised Land) were in God's favor, so he refused even to say the words. To curse the Children of Israel would have been entirely out of character with the Lord's will. It would also have been entirely futile.

We are a people living under a baptismal covenant. So, for us everything we do is "in the name of the Lord," It's not just our words but our actions that come under judgment here. Taking the Lord's name in vain might be a function of our speech or of our activities.

(4) Remember the Sabbath to keep it holy. "So, God blessed the seventh day and hallowed it, because on it God rested from all his work which he had done . . .," Literally, Sabbath is "seventh" or Saturday, for Jewish people, from sundown Friday

through sundown Saturday. (since a day is reckoned as starting at sundown on the previous day). You will recall at the crucifixion, (Friday afternoon) following his death, Jesus' body was hurriedly removed from the cross and placed in the tomb. It had to be done before sundown in observance of Sabbath regulations. In fact it was such a hurry-up job, the women had to wait until Sunday morning to go back to the tomb to take care of the body in accordance with their burial customs, which, of course gave rise to the discovery of the empty tomb.

"Sabbath" was also extended to the seventh year. For example in cultivating a field you could take a crop for six years, then you were supposed to let the land lie fallow for the seventh year. There were many such extensions including the year of jubilee. (50th year [7times7+1] at which time all debts were canceled, all slaves were set free etc, and everybody set up for a fresh beginning). At least that was the idea. Now in our time, given the nature of commerce, travel, international communication and so on it would be next to impossible for anyone to observe this commandment literally. But we should recognize the sense of it and strive for some way to observe its point to our own health and well-being.

I remember as a kid there was still a lot of cultural pressure to observe the Sabbath. If you had a factory job, you had to abide by the factory's hours. But half of the people still lived on a family farm, and farmers observed the day of rest. There was some fear of what the neighbors would think if you were seen working the field on Sunday. So, there was quite a lot of sneaking around, some gossip, and not a little guilt in the neighborhood.

The second half of the fifties saw me in seminary in Vancouver B.C. The social pressure in Canada to observe the Sabbath was even greater than in the U.S. And in Vancouver (as in Seattle) it rains all the time. So, it was a big temptation to cover some outdoor chores (wash the car; mow the lawn) on a sunny Sunday afternoon. Well, it was one of those sunny Sundays. We had been to church that morning, but now it was afternoon and the grass was already too high and thick. So, with a small tug of guilt on my heart, I dragged the mower out of the shed and around to the front yard. It was a power mower, reel type, with a grass catcher

on the back. I cranked it up and started cutting out the perim-
eter.

The yard was fenced all around; no reason for foot traffic in
there. Yet on my first pass I spotted something in the grass to my
left reflecting the sun right into my eyes. I passed on and came
around again. On the second pass there it was again still reflecting the sun directly into my eyes. It was still a little to my left,
so, once more I ignored it. It was the third or fourth pass, and
I had forgotten the annoying reflector, when the mower passed
directly over the place and flipped the object up into the grass
catcher, where it lay, still reflecting the sun directly into my
eyes. (The grass was piling into the catcher and should have buried the thing.) It now had my attention.

So I stopped, reached into the pile of grass and retrieved it.
It was a charm from a child's bracelet, like new except where
the mower blade had nicked it; originally one of a set of ten. It
read "4 :Remember the Sabbath, to keep it Holy." I still have no
idea how it got there, in the middle of a fenced yard on a street
with virtually no foot traffic, or how, with all that thick grass that
thing managed to stay on the surface and focus the sun right in
my eyes. Anyway, I quit and put the mower away, and I still have
that charm. Again we are taking the view that the commandment
is not an arbitrary rule set over against our flawed nature, but a
revelation from God describing our true nature.

(5) Honor your father and your mother. "Well", you might
challenge, "if my father and my mother are despicable people,
totally evil or without redeeming value, does this mean that I'm
to treat them with the respect normally reserved for fine upstanding citizens? And would that not make me a hypocrite?" Remember, we are trying to abstract from the literal sense of these
commandments to a more philosophical understanding of what's
behind them. So considered, I'd translate this one to something
like "respect your roots" or your ancestry, or your tribe (or race
or nationality). When black Americans in the 60s, came up with
the cheer "Black is beautiful." they were responding to this
commandment. Being white, I didn't get it at first. So my initial
response was "Well, of course black people are beautiful–most of
them, same as white people–same as others."

Then it struck me. As a culture this was not what we were saying. Department store manikins were white. Models posing for catalogues were white. Little black girls, for the most part, had to play with white dolls. Our culture was shouting out "white is beautiful, and what's more, it's normal." So, there's plenty for us to ponder in the fifth commandment no matter how you feel about the couple who produced you.

(6, 8 & 9) You shall not murder, steal or be a false witness. So, the final three! I will sum them up in the words from our baptismal covenant: Respect the dignity of every human being. That doesn't leave anyone out. We are pledged to respect everyone in terms of their lives, their possessions and their names. And we can do that. I'll expound on one example: capitol punishment. I know some evil people are out there, but I'm not talking about them, I'm talking about us. In capitol punishment, no one's human dignity escapes. Look at the faces of the victims, people you see on the evening news, shouting for revenge, fists clinched, faces contorted, hatred in their eyes -- no dignity there. Think of those who volunteer for the firing squad, to administer the death penalty. I know they don't have to do it; it's an all volunteer operation. But why should we condone such a system?

What about the guy who pulls the switch or springs the trap door or those who are required to witness? There's no dignity there for anyone. Why should we put up with procedures with absolutely no redeeming value? The only argument I've heard for the death penalty is that it is a deterrent. But I have never heard of a study that bears that out. The studies I have heard of refute that argument, and today we are about the only civilized country that still supports capitol punishment. But our baptismal covenant says it best: "Respect the dignity of every human being."

Again, these are not rules I am expected to try hard to obey, but a mirror of true, whole humanity; a revelation standing over us in our sinfulness. Here is the way it is set forth in Deuteronomy (30: 11-14). For this commandment which I command you this day is not in heaven, that you should say, "Who will go up for us to heaven, and bring it to us, that we may hear it and do it? Neither is it beyond the sea, that you should say, "Who will go over the sea for us, and bring it to us that we may hear it and do it?"

But the word is very near you; it is in your mouth and in your heart, so that you can do it; it is not a whole humanity that I can eventually attain to. (If I could, I'd end up boasting about it and blow it.) It's a human nature we can grow into as we surrender our lives to the work of Christ within us. The commandments cry out, not for obedience, but for grace.

SEND OFF

Final Homily of the Term

So, our final Sunday together for this academic year; then we're off on our various summer adventures, living out our vocations along the way. And how do we do that? Well, we are not without guidance even from today's readings. This, from the Book of Acts for instance: "for the Lord has commanded us, saying, I have set you to be a light to the nations, so that you may bring salvation to the ends of the earth." That's the mission. At the close of the day, will we be graded on how well we've done? Well, not in the manner you've grown accustomed to in recent years. But John's Gospel gives us a pretty good idea of what to look for; By this everyone will know that you are my disciples, if you have love for one another.

To be a light to the nations! That's not exactly a challenge to us one by one; it's a group charge-a charge to the whole church. Individually, we have our baptismal vows and those are incredibly important. But collectively, to be a "light to the nations" we must also pay attention to the disciplines of our corporate discipleship. And those disciplines have to do with liturgy, music, ceremonial, architecture and the like. In Wyoming, over the years, we have been working on renewal in all those aspects of our personal and corporate life.

The name Ernie Southcott is not one that many of you will be familiar with. Ernie Southcott was a very popular English evangelist of the 50s and the 60s. He was the rector of a large Anglican church in one of England's huge urban slums. Somehow he revitalized and brought that church to life. I had heard of him before I went to seminary in 1957. My seminary was The Anglican Theological College on the campus of U.B.C. in

Vancouver, British Columbia. It wasn't long after arriving there that I discovered that Ernie had a brother who was rector of one of the suburban churches in the Vancouver metro-area. Needless to say, I made it a point to meet this guy and attend his church a couple of times. So it was that I first met Ernie. He was making one of his frequent tours of North America and had stopped by for a visit with his brother.

Some eight or nine years later -- by this time, an appointed officer of our national church in New York City -- I found Ernie making another of his North American tours. Someone had scheduled him to stop by our office for an airing of his experience before returning to England. I was one of the small group of staff members invited to sit at Ernie's feet and share in his observations of the Episcopal Church, U.S.A.

He started off by setting forth a basic theory of renewal. The way to generate new insights and ideas concerning church renewal, he suggested, was: 1) do the familiar thing (eg. liturgy) in a wildly unusual setting. Or, 2) do something off the wall in an old familiar setting; Then, in each case, pay attention to what happens. He went on to observe that in his tour of the Episcopal Church U.S.A. (late 60s remember) he saw five huge blocks to church renewal: the altar, the pews, the Book of Common Prayer, the organ and the building. Well, that didn't leave much out.

The altar, because we had it bolted to the east wall; you couldn't get around it, you couldn't get behind it, and the officiant was stuck with reading the service with his (and it was his) back to the congregation.

Next were the pews, fastened to the floor. So the people sat there like lines on a printed page staring at the backs of the heads of all those in front, with those who sat behind completely invisible.

Then there was the 1928 Book of Common Prayer with its inflexible liturgy set, not in the language of the people but in beautiful, 400 year old, poetic, Elizabethan English with obscure phrases barely intelligible even to educated adults, let alone to youngsters of the day.

The organ-pipes and console in many churches was, as were
the altar and pews, a built in, permanent fixture. Even when
we provided for a more modest instrument such as a reed or
an electronic organ the attitude remained the same. This instrument was so good how could you improve upon it? In other
words, we were, in the late 60s, stuck with the organ. We were
blocked (Ernie's point) from trying something else; blocked
from doing something wild and different in this old familiar
space; blocked from renewal.

Finally, the building; the reredos, the stained glass windows,
the altar rail, clearly all designed for all of the above; so awesome, so holy, we forgot that all God's creation is holy. The
nave with its pews, row upon row; the choir and the organ near
the crossing, effectively barring the people from getting too
close to the holy of holies; and finally, the altar somewhere
over the horizon nailed to the east wall, clergy and acolytes
mumbling with their backs to the congregation. How could you
do anything else with such a space? Renewal did indeed seem
impossible.

I don't know where Ernie Southcott was over the next forty
years, but those years saw a revolution in all of the above. Here
and there a few brave souls began fooling around with guitars,
flutes, cymbals and other strange (in church settings) musical
instruments, and, at least some of the people seemed to appreciate the variety and flexibility. Then someone remembered
that the offerings of the people include the bread and the
wine-not just the money; it includes our flesh and blood-our
lives and vocations. So the bread and wine became part of the
presentation at the holy table.

Now all this creativity didn't seem to work with an altar
beyond the horizon, so some brave soul ventured to set up a
table in the midst of the choir; awkward, clumsy, crowded-but
a start. Soon another somewhat more venturous contributor set
up an altar right in the crossing-right in the midst of the people. Is nothing sacred any more? Soon, we were fooling around
with trial liturgies, preparing ourselves for the 1979 Prayer

Book. Then we awakened one morning to find women serving
as priests and bishops. It was a struggle getting there, but once
there it didn't just feel natural; it felt like ordained ministry
was much more whole-complete-as a result of making it inclusive. Depending on one's perspectives, it was an exciting time .
. . or a total disaster.

Eventually, of course, the architects began to pick up on
all this; first by rearranging the furniture and redecorating.
However, they soon started getting ideas about reordering the
space. Why not, for example, arrange things so that people
could gather in a circle as they might be inclined to do for a
service in the park; gather in a circle around the table, or the
font, or the musicians, depending on the action.

Here and there churches were remodeled or created from
the start with flexible seating, movable fixtures, ingenious
lighting-all designed to maximize flexibility and support liturgical innovation. And so it went through the 70s, the 80s, and
the 90s. Massive adjustments we now take for granted. Ernie
Southcott's five huge blocks had been severely compromised.

So now, here we are, the 20th century behind us. We have
struggled through its wars, its social upheavals; as a church
we are facing up to racism, sexism, homophobia, and a host of
other cultural challenges. I'm not saying that we have a perfect
track record, but as those things go, the Episcopal Church has
stayed the course with the best of them and set an example for
all. Along the way we have lost a few souls committed to another course, but we have gained many looking for a Christian
community with a vision, with conviction and resolve, and we
are that community. And we are today a stronger, more focused
community in mission as a result of our experience.

Anyway, here we go, to be a light to the nations, to live
out our baptismal covenant on our journeys this summer. So,
how do you think it will go? It's going to go just fine! I had an
advance peek at the grades. And I know already that you are
disciples of Jesus-passed with flying colors. And how do I know?
I can see the great love that you have for one another.

BEING, HAVING, DOING

Baptimsal Covenant II

Last February, as we were just getting into the new year, I preached on the Baptismal Covenant. It seemed like a good way to initiate a new relationship; all get started on the same page so to speak. At that time I went through examples and illustrations from real life, to interpret each of these promises for our time and circumstances. Now I'm going to ask you to turn once more to the Covenant (page 304 BCP) The part at the bottom of the page that starts out "Will you . . " We'll read this together after the sermon as part of the Prayers of the People

This time however, I'll address a different issue. Our response on these pages is "I will with God's help." But how do we do that? That will be my topic this afternoon. The readings today are actually from proper 13C, scheduled for mid August, but substituted for today because that's where they fit for us.

I'll first call your attention to Ecclesiastes. The small portion we read for today is a very good sampling of the character of the whole book. Our unknown author refers to himself as the "teacher" or the "preacher." And he takes on the persona of King Solomon, a person of unprecedented wealth with a reputation for great wisdom. I don't know about wealth, but this writer is indeed a person of considerable wisdom. His thoughts run deep and his observations are certainly not those of a fool. His conclusions however are conclusions of despair-cynicism. Life to him is an absurdity; total futility. The word our translator uses is "vanity;" not just empty, as in pointless, but offensively empty as in promises not kept; pride and hope trampled on "vanity of vanities." And this is the tone of the whole book. Some scholars wonder why we keep a piece such as this in our collection of Holy Scriptures; there is nothing in here to offset this terrible pessimism. But others say it is a voice that needs to be heard.

Psalm 49 is a good companion piece to Ecclesiastes. This author claims wisdom, but, as in Ecclesiastes, expresses deep cynicism.

"For we see that the wise die also; like the dull and stupid they perish and leave their wealth to those who come after them. Their graves shall be their homes forever; their dwelling place from generation to generation, though they call the lands after their own names. Even though honored, they cannot live forever; they are like the beasts that perish."

Then (in the Gospel) we have the parable of the farmer with the barn problem. He doesn't pray about this problem; he talks to himself. He doesn't share his abundance; he seeks a way to save it all. To himself: "What shall I do, for I have nowhere to store my crop. I will do this, I will pull down my barns and build larger ones; and I will say to my soul, 'soul you have ample goods laid up for many years; relax, eat, drink and be merry.'" This is not the deep thinking of the preacher, it's the musings of a fool. But the fool ends up in the same place; life is futility; life is absurd; vanity of vanities. The preacher and the psalmist, with all their wisdom, see it clearly. The farmer hasn't discovered it yet. And in his ignorance and foolishness he may never.

So, what can we say about these "wise" fools? Where is their error; that makes life so empty, absurd, vain for them? Theirs is one of the most basic of human errors -- they confuse having and doing with being. Hear again the preacher: "It is an unhappy business that God has given to human beings to be busy with. I saw all the deeds that are done under the sun, all is vanity and a chasing after the wind," . . . all about doing. Or the farmer: "I will do this, I will pull down all my barns and build larger ones and then I will store all my grain and my goods," . . . all about having. The question of being, never occurs to either one of them.

Recall the story of Moses and the burning bush. Moses says, who shall I say sent me? And the voice comes back, I Am that I Am . . . tell them that 'I Am sent you.' That's apparently the best we can make of it in English. Scholars say that in the Hebrew it seems to represent all forms of the verb "to be." We might be inclined to say that it is the voice of Being Itself . . .of Ultimate Being. The Ultimate "isness" of God. And if we are "to be" (never mind what), our being will be grounded in Ultimate Being; and that's the only way it can work.

We can never in a dozen lifetimes have, gain, accumulate, own enough wealth, property, stuff to be someone. We can never accomplish, succeed, do something (good, evil or indifferent) to be someone. We can't create our being with our having and doing. It can't work that way. Being has to come first.

Carlyle Marney, an early Baptist contemporary of mine in mutual ministry development, puts it eloquently: The Christian faith rests neither on doing or having. Salvation by faith is salvation by grace–an affirmation of being as being. It means a willingness to be as one is without any direct object. He is as he is, warts and all. To be is to be, even without arms and legs; one could almost say without mind. To be is to be without defense, possession, excuse, power, energy, or will. It is never to be what. The objects all drop off. We are stripped; no harness, no titles, no havings, no gotness, no doings. Being is just being. And this is where Christ meets me -- just as I am.

We hide behind our having and our doing. We misuse these verbs, says Marney, and most of us have missed the point. He goes on: A teenaged paraplegic, who has no hands or legs to use, little voice, no way to be mobile, and really almost nothing but a mind, asked by some ill-made social worker if she wouldn't as soon be done with it all, answers: "I wouldn't have missed being for anything."

"Yet having and doing have their place," says Marney, "to be religious involves what I do with what I have." False as this is, literally, there is something to this. Doing and having are inescapable functions of being, but they are not being. And they are results, effects, of being, not supports of being. Our religious doing and having rests on our being, not otherwise.

Marney illustrates: "I heard, sometime in the afternoon, that shrewd manipulation from outside had cost him his lifetime business and several million dollars. In the early evening I dropped by just to see what, if anything, I could be. He was sitting in pajamas on his bed, eating a ripe banana, smoking his perennial pipe, and reading the New Testament (something about barns, I think he said). I went on home."

Christianity is a way of life, says Marney, and it is priesthood. I am a mediating man, expecting to meet Christ everywhere I go: Christianity "is not a possession, it is being possessed. Not a seizure, it is being seized. Not a closure of the fist, it is an opening of the hand and heart. Not propositions to which one must assent, it offers relations which one accepts. It is a willingness to be, not an urge to have. And above all, the Christian being is a hope, a hope of having not yet arrived. A hope that the last word is not "frustration," that "more to follow" still goes at the end of every page. This hope is the confidence that my obedience and hungry unfilledness, my fears and questings do matter and do participate in a coming kingdom that matters.

So, our response in the covenant is, "I will with God's help." But, I'm telling you, you will not, not by trying real hard! You cannot as an act of the will because it is not, first of all a matter of doing. It is the same point I made to you some time ago about the Decalogue. The sense of the commandments is not that we should try real hard to obey. We can't come at it that way. The tenth commandment says we shall not covet. So if I covet obedience to the commandments, I've already blown it! Obedience to the law or living into our baptismal covenant is first of all a matter of Being. When we get being straight then proper doing will flow from it.

You might recall a story I told you last year, of the lad who was struggling with the tenth commandment. "I can't help it," he said, "When my friend gets a new model plane, I do covet it." We continued to work on it until finally I saw his eyes light up and he said, "Oh, I see what you mean Fr. Wilson; you mean that if I really love my friend, then when he gets something new I'll feel good for him and then I will be obeying the commandment without even thinking about it."

"You got it" I said. So, commandment or covenant, it is not, first of all, a matter of doing; it is first off, a matter of becoming; of growing, and becoming so grounded in God's grace that doing and having come into place as proper functions of being, not as foundations.

INTROSPECTION

Me and the Pharisee

   Self awareness is certainly one of our greatest gifts; a rich, rich blessing indeed. But it is also humanity's foremost curse and challenge. According to the creation narratives there was no self-awareness, originally, in the Garden of Eden. And as we can see today there is apparently no self-awareness in the animal kingdom around us. The coming of self-consciousness in the creation narratives is seen as a curse. Before the fall our ancestors in Eden were naked and didn't know it.

   But when Eve took it upon herself to bring the knowledge of good and evil into this garden of perfection, a whole new story begin to unfold. Adam and Eve were naked and they knew it and they had to hide from God. In other words they were guilty. And God threw them out of paradise. So we've had to live with the gift of self awareness ever since. But for me at least, it is indeed a gift, a blessing. Who wants to go back to some primal jungle living as stupid apes, surviving from day to day and thinking we are in paradise? Not me! Praise the Lord for Eve! I'll take self consciousness and forge ahead. I know that that involves sin and guilt and the need for repentance and grace and all that. But I would not choose to go back.

   It can, however get pretty complicated. For example, I can smile at an amusing incident–I can laugh out loud at a good joke, but point a camera at me, and I can do neither. That's why I don't allow weddings to become photo ops for the camera gangs. They destroy subjectivity. The couple can't be totally "there" for each other; they can't be "in" the action and be observers of it at the same time. A wedding is a time for subjectivity, not a time for posing. (They can do all the posing they want after we're finished with the service).

I mentioned the complexity; the complexity lies in the several layers of objectivity we can sometimes create. Let's say I decide to go outside and play "fetch" with the dog. That'll be just fine with the dog. So we go out and I throw and the dog "fetches." That can go on for quite a while; we simply enjoy being there together; total subjectivity.

But I can change the dynamics quite a bit if I become objective; that is, self conscious, in that setting. I can leave that immediate relationship and, in my mind, go apart (to the other side of the yard, let's say) and from there observe me and the dog playing fetch. If I do that, the subjective spell that we were in is broken, and the dog will know it. But I can take it another layer. Suppose that I now (in my mind, of course) go up overhead to that cloud where I can observe the whole picture. I can see me and the dog playing fetch. I can also see me, the observer watching the play. But I'm still another layer away. I'm the observer watching the observer. By this time the dog will have gotten disgusted and left. But that's where self awareness takes us.

Let me give you a real life example. Many years ago, just before going to Seminary, I lived in western Idaho and I was running a small propane gas business. At that time we had a large commercial hot plate that we kept on hand for the convenience of our customers. If a church group or a grange or any one else for that matter wanted to borrow it for a pancake supper or some other occasion, all they had to do was make a phone call to reserve it. They could pick it up as scheduled, return it later, and we would supply the gas to boot. It was a fairly popular community service.

In those days we got some heavy rains and a neighboring community was flooded. I heard about it via the grapevine; several families had to find temporary shelter, others were trying to feed people in the local school etc. It was a rural community, so we had customers in the area. Anyway I just happened to think of the hot plate. They could probably use it. So

I got in touch with a local contact and offered to bring it over. "Yes" they could definitely use it. So I loaded it up in my pick up along with a full bottle of gas and headed out. It was over a hill into another valley, then on toward the flooded town.

Now I want to emphasize that all this was fully spontaneous, totally unselfconscious action on my part . . . so far. But I wasn't more than two miles down the road when the thought hit me; "Hey, this will be really good PR for us." With that, innocence was lost. The offering was now tainted, and I was guilty and knew it. Objectivity had reared its ugly head; subjectivity was lost. I felt dirty. What had started out as a perfectly innocent, worthy offering was now soiled. Nothing but a simple "flip" in my brain and the meaning of what I was doing was suddenly switched from a selfless deed to a self-serving promotional tactic. Well, I couldn't turn back now; they still needed the thing, so, I went on. Within the next mile or so another thought came to mind. They will probably think that PR is the reason I'm doing this anyway. Double whammy. Like the picture of Norman Rockwell painting a picture of himself, painting a picture of himself painting a picture, Etc.

Well, today we have the story of the Pharisee and the tax collector coming into the temple to pray. Remember that in this culture the Pharisee is the good guy; a religious figure in the community, a highly respected citizen. And the tax collector is scum. However, to make his point, Jesus reverses the roles. As Jesus tells it, our inclination is to side with the tax collector. So, I'll play it through that way. (But Jesus doesn't really know how many layers of this objectivity I can get to.)

I (tax collector) and the Pharisee approach the temple about the same time. I (humble man that I am) defer, and he goes in first. I watch: A pillar of the church; a major contributor to the budget; active in community affairs; highly respected by all. One who leads an exemplary life. That's all I need. He proudly walks right up the center aisle to the altar rail, genuflects, then stands there looking heavenward with the sun streaming in through a side window forming a halo like effect around his head.

I look for a dark corner in one of the rear pews, find it and quietly slink into place, bow my head. I don't dare look at him; just reminds me of how bad I really am. I beat my breast, mouth my confession. Then it happens-just as Jesus promised. The burden is lifted. I know that I am all right with God. Because of his love and forgiving grace I'm a free man, a forgiven human being.

I begin to get up-free to go down to my house justified. Then I notice him, still at it. Who does he think he is? Doesn't he know about grace? No, just about good works! Well, thank God I'm not like that Pharisee – self-righteous, pious, "holier than thou," do gooder. But with that, I'm exactly like that Pharisee-and I know it! All the guilt returns; back to my dark corner, back on my knees. through it all again. And again, confession, repentance; the burden is lifted. So, once more I prepare to stand and go down to my house justified. But as I stand, I look back again-at that damn Pharisee-but now with a little more understanding.

Well, thank God, At least I know how it works!

THE CROWD

Zacchaeus' Winning Day

I'm going to ask you to picture this city. It's a real town, so I'll try to describe in enough detail that you can get a reasonably good picture of it in your mind's eye. The city is in a rich valley with a river flowing through. The people export a lot of the produce of this valley. In fact, the city is something of a crossroads in this part of the world. Caravans come and go. People exchange ideas and wares as foreigners and travelers mix it up with the locals. The poor people live in shacks on the flats bordering the river downstream. They do not generally have any plumbing, so the river fills this need for most of them. But let's go on up stream from the main business district. Here the valley broadens, and we see the larger homes, gardens and orchards of the well-to-do. I should hasten to add however, that while they have their share of poor folk in this town, on the whole this is a prosperous community. The setting is the middle-east and the time, about 2000 years ago.

Now park that view on the side for a minute, while we create a parallel picture. This time I'll ask you to see the crowd, the unruly mob in the street, the restless, unpredictable mob that is everywhere. See them following Moses; crowding, complaining, bitching; never satisfied. For them nothing is right, nothing is acceptable. "Give us something to eat–we're sick and tired of this manna. We want meat and fresh water. Why did you bring us out here; to die on the trail?" It's the generic mob. We see them everywhere. See them following John the Baptist; "Save us! Do some miracle for us!" They are not bad people. They are just ordinary folk; tradesmen, farmers, homemakers, like you and me. But when people come together as a mob, something happens to them; they are not just ordinary people; they are a mob.

See them again following Jesus everywhere. Down at the sea

he had to get some distance from them in order to be able to stand up and preach. So he got in a boat, pushed off from shore, stood up in the boat and held forth. Along the road they crowded around him so he could hardly walk. A woman forced her way through the crowd; if she could only touch his robe; maybe that would do it. And she did, and that did it; she was healed. Jesus stopped, "who touched me?" he asked his followers.

"Who touched you? Are you kidding? Look at this mob!" Then on a grassy hillside, "how are we going to feed all these people?" "Well, what do we have to work with?" "Okay, have them sit down."

Another time he escaped into a building to get some relief from the pressing mob. Some of them climbed up on the roof and lowered their comrade down through the roof nearly on top of Jesus. And so it went, the crowd, everywhere the fickle crowd. Then came the triumphal entry into Jerusalem, while the mob cheered and shouted hosannas. Shortly thereafter hear them again (same crowd remember) calling for his blood. "Crucify him-crucify him."

Now we'll go back to the city. The city is Jericho. The river is the Jordan. Now add the crowd -- same old crowd -- they will soon be headed up to Jerusalem. Our story focuses on one man; the chief tax collector hated by everyone, known by everyone as a sinner, a cheat, an opportunist, and of course a wealthy man. He had everything and he had nothing. He had a beautiful wife and he had one of those big estates up the river from town, with a swimming pool, extensive orchards and gardens, servants to look after things and a high fence all around (he needed that for security). And he had nothing; no friends, no respect, no social life; he was alone, empty, and lonely; desperate to make some sense out of his miserable life.

The crowd, by contrast, at least as seen by the crowd, fine, upstanding, respectable people. Jesus called that man a son of Abraham. Think of that linage for a minute; Abraham, the liar, Jacob, the thief, Moses, the murderer, his brother, the crafter of idols; Rahab, the harlot; Ruth, stranger of Moab, David, the adulterer. Well, when you look at the record there's plenty of sin to go around. But they were not thinking of that.

Several years ago I had a funeral for a family I didn't know. A woman came to me to make arrangements. The funeral would be for her father. I could find no one in the congregation who knew these people. However, (the woman explained), the family had once been associated with the parish. They were dropouts. Now, I'm not interested in chalking up one more pastoral service for the sake of the parochial report that I'll fill out come year's end. But the time of death calls for a little special pastoral sensitivity. So I heard the lady out and agreed to do the service. They had in fact been part of the parish years ago. She could tell me of her experience as a youngster, and that of her father who had once served on the vestry, so I officiated.

After the service I dropped into the residence where the family had gathered to see if there was anything of a pastoral nature that I should pick up on. I got my cup of coffee and visited with the woman; the only person there that I knew. She told me of her early association with the church, how her family had been active in a number of ways. She finished up with, "But I outgrew my need for that kind of stuff years ago." Then added, (knowingly and with a sly grin on her face), "After, all I'm no miserable sinner." Well, I thought, not much for me to do here. And I excused myself.

She was one of those nice people from the crowd. I guess there has to be at least a touch of sainthood in people for them to know that they are miserable sinners and in need of salvation.

Anyway, that's the story of how one thoroughly wretched, despicable, hated man in his desperate loneliness sought to see God and was scooped up by God.

And his sins which were like scarlet became white as snow; and the crowd went on grumbling and complaining, totally unaware that salvation had come to one house that day!

THE WORLD IS COMING TO AN END

Standing Before the Judgment Seat

I thought about starting our service this afternoon by marching in with a placard held overhead, The World is Coming to the End It is, you know. Both Science and Theology speculate about end times. Even Robert Frost, the New England poet ponders the issue in this tongue-in-cheek ditty.

Some say the world will end in fire
Some say, in ice
From what I've tasted of desire
I hold with those who favor fire
But if it had to perish twice
I think I know enough of hate
To say that for destruction ice
Is also great–and would suffice

The speculation in Science hangs on the question of the total mass of the universe. If it is great enough, then gravity will take over, the expansion of the universe will grind to a halt and the whole thing will begin to collapse into a big crunch. But if the mass is not that great the expansion will continue until all is cold and empty. So, take your pick; the end is a big crunch or a whimper.

Religious writing speculating on the end times is referred to as Apocalyptic Literature. The Book of Revelation is a leading example. In the end (that's what "apocalyptic" means) the good will prevail, evil will be put down, and the Kingdom of God will be fully realized. So, you see, bottom line, "The world is coming to the end" is really Good News. But, meantime the struggle continues.

This Sunday also marks the end of the church year. It's called Christ the King Sunday. But notice the ambivalence;

The Gospel for this Sunday is Luke's account of the crucifixion. The king hangs on the cross! Fairly apocalyptic I'd say. On the other hand his kingship is affirmed. Hear again the criminal, Jesus, remember me when you come into your kingdom. And Jesus' response, Truly I tell you, today you will be with me in paradise. I suppose there is good reason for us to feel ambivalent about the world coming to the end. Not that we are likely to be around to experience it. But still, just the idea. Yet still again, the promises: Behold I make all things new. It really is a total victory; thoroughly Good News. We should be looking foreword to it in high anticipation.

I spent the month of July, 1965 at Claremont College, Los Angeles in a workshop led by Saul Alinski, a very controversial community organizer. The workshop had been sponsored by our national church and I was one of about 30 people invited to attend. It was certainly one of the best educational experiences of my life. Alinski was a criminologist who had been associated with the University of Chicago. He was also a highly educated person, deeply rooted in the defining documents of the founding of American democracy. He was a contemporary of John L. Lewis, the great labor organizer. However Alinski was interested in organizing neighborhoods to take part in the politics of their city. In certain principals, it had some overlap with labor organizing. His initial target was a Chicago neighborhood known as "Back of the Yards," the locale of the meat packing industry. This was in the days of prohibition and mob rule in Chicago. Back of the Yards was an urban area of mostly poor, Roman Catholic ethnic people; Poles, Italians, etc. who were fiercely loyal to their own local ethnic parish and incredibly competitive from church to church.

It was an era in our history when people were expected to attend church, and members of the mob were, of course, among the faithful. So, Alinski set out to organize these ethnic church groups to attack City Hall and win some neighborhood concessions, such as better trash pick up, improved street maintenance and the like. This set him at odds with the rich bosses in the meat packing industry who were exploiting the neighborhood. So the battle lines were drawn. At one point, one night, someone took a shot at Alinski. Maybe it was just to scare him, maybe they simply missed. But he had to put a stop to that foolishness.

Now Saul was well known in the mob. He was trying to understand how the criminal mind worked, so he hung out with them a lot to the point where they trusted him; he was no snitch. So he contacted one well known member, a hit man, whose mug shot frequented the papers; Then he made an appointment with one of the big shots in the industry, and showed up for the appointment in the company of his friend, the hit man.

Alinski opened the conversation with a report on his attempted assassination. (Nothing was mentioned of the accompanying mob member who just sat there "for effect"). "Oh no, now who would want to kill you?" asked the CEO.

"I don't know" responded Saul. "But I just thought you should know that if they do get me, you're next!"

"Why me?" stammered the CEO, "I didn't have anything to do with it."

"I didn't say you did" said Saul, "But I wanted you to know that if they get me, you're next."

The stammering continued, the two guests excused themselves and left. The mob member had never opened his mouth. But that was the end of the shooting. And that's the kind of character we had in Saul Alinski.

One time in class someone asked Saul if he should finally win his way; that is, achieve fair play and honesty in all neighborhoods everywhere, what then would he turn his attention to? Immediately he shot back, "Music and art, which is why we were put here in the first place." He had obviously given that one some considerable thought. I greatly respected his response.

I'll give you another little vignette. Many years ago an associate of mine took a short sabbatical to go to Germany and study under the great Karl Barth. Karl Barth, at the time, was a well known theologian and New Testament scholar. (There were many world-recognized theologians in Germany in the first half of the last century; Germany was exporting theological scholarship even as Hitler was gaining power and conquering Europe.) Anyway, this was before Hitler's time; the exchange of students was common, and many took advantage of an opportunity to sit at the feet of the masters and soak up some wisdom. I don't know what Barth was teaching at the time, but he had an international group of students, and the occasion was well publicized.

Barth had a profound sense of the apocalyptic character of the promise of the Kingdom. This from Barth's commentary on Paul's Letter to the Romans: "We shall all stand before the judgment Seat of God." (Then, Barth, aside,) "The Lord, as we have just heard, is the Judge over life and over death. The implications of this must be thoroughly examined and applied. Because we SHALL all stand before the judgment seat . . . it must follow that we all, being what we ARE, ARE standing before the judgment seat, some of us in our strength, some of us in our weakness. Terrified before the final, unheard-of fact that we are the Lord's, we all in some fashion or other . . . venture upon some attempt to be righteous in the presence of God."

Of course, newspaper folk, (who don't particularly understand the faith, let alone graduate work in Theology), are constantly hanging around famous people hoping for a scoop or some tid-bit to craft into an article that might get some attention. At one point in the proceedings a young female reporter managed to get the attention of the great scholar, "Doctor Barth, if you could have your greatest wish granted, what would that be?"

Without hesitation, he snapped back, "That this damned world come to an end tomorrow". She huffed and scurried, gathered up her stuff, and beat it out of the room slamming the door behind her. He turned back to his students, a twinkle in his eye and a sly grin on his face, "They really don't understand us do they"?

WORD INTO FLESH

On Preaching: II Advent

A Sunday sermon follow-up on a Saturday preaching course

Large and small corporations, manufacturing and marketing enterprises, CEOs and labor groups all stake their names and corporate reputations on it. Government agencies, professional associations in Law, Medicine and Religion all design codes of ethics around it. Even little children, nearly as soon as they gain a command of the language, show evidence of an innate sense of the inviolability or sacredness of it. It is a matter of highest honor and esteem in heaven and on earth, and yes, God himself is totally at one with it.

What is "it"? "It" is WORD, the most powerful instrument at our disposal. I can give you my Word (called a pledge). I can stand on my Word. (And if I don't, I'm a liar or worse.) I can withhold my Word. (And leave you hanging and me impotent. The influence I might have exerted for good is lost forever.) And you all know the power of the Word, a Word spoken in haste in a fit of rage, the soothing and comforting Word of a friend when trouble looms larger than life. The careless Word out of touch with what the other is going through. And have you ever faced the disappointment, the hurt and sense of betrayal of the small child who looks at you accusingly and says, "But you gave your word"?

Fred Craddock has this to say of Word: "In some sense, all a man has is his word. In certain moments of his life he is asked to give it. If in those moments he is separated from his word, then he is separated from himself. He may gain many other words, big important words, words that will get votes, win compliments, elicit applause, gain members, or sell real estate, but having lost his word, he himself is lost." Words have a power all of their own. Of course, I can offer different kinds of words:

words of encouragement and blessing, words that can build up and support. And I can offer words that destroy or demoralize and tear down. But once a word is spoken, that word goes forth to carry out the errand contained in the word. I can't call it back; its job, for good or ill, is already accomplished.

I said that "it" was a characteristic of business, CEOs, professionals and many others. Here I'll draw on my bridges between theology and the practice of management. What we call "word," is, in the business community, referred to as "Policy." Policy is the Word of the business or professional practitioner. Notice the parallels: Policy spells out the values of the enterprise, but in operational terms. The Company President might say "We insist on fair hiring and promotional practices throughout this organization." And to that I'd have to say "mere rhetoric; what does 'fair' mean?" Fair is a value term, not a policy. And that might be okay for the PR purposes of this firm, but not for the people actually charged with the hiring and promoting of personnel. For them you need real policy. "In our hiring and promoting practices we do not consider age, gender or sexual orientation, race or ethnic roots, religious affiliation or lack thereof. On the other hand we do allow some edge to one who is already an employee of the firm with a good track record." Now, if I am the head of a department and considering taking on additional staff, I have some real policy to guide me. I know what the word of the company is on the matter.

So, the policy of the company or agency is a direct parallel to the word of a friend. Jay Forrester of M.I.T. says that: (1) Policy must afford a certain amount of freedom of interpretation and application. Where this is not the case, policy is experienced as suppressive. (2) It must be accessible. If it is not known or if it is brought to bear after the action, it is experienced as frustrating. (3) Policy, in so far as possible, ought to be mutually agreed to. Where it is imposed for the benefit of the imposer it is most antagonizing. (4) Finally, it should be internally consistent. If not it is merely confusing.

Now, of course we could say all these things about a person's word. We expect a person's word to permit a little latitude for give and take among well meaning people. We hope that the other guy is open so we can see where he is coming from. We don't appreciate the other imposing his or her standards, beliefs or causes on us. And we appreciate it when the other comes across as consistent and reliable. Now, what can we say about a business whose policy meets these standards or about a person whose word stands up to these principals? We might be inclined to say "Now there's a company (or a person) you can trust." And we picked up our clues from the policy or word. Clear signals (policy or word) invite and promote trust among people.

Now, if word is such a big concept here on earth, what are we to make of the Word of God? Well, at least all that we've said about the word that circulates among people must be also applicable to God's Word. God's Word ought to be comprehensible, understandable. It should be internally consistent, worthy of trust (actually we would probably say 'faith') and, of course, the power of God must stand behind it; if not, what's the point? And, as a matter of fact, one of the common, persistent and consistent terms in the Hebrew and Christian scriptures is Word.

The first chapter of Genesis opens with an extensive account of how God spoke "Let it be. And it was so. And God saw that it was good." For six days God acted, and on the seventh, God rested. The Word of God went forth into the chaos, and the Word of God brought forth order, form, meaning and beauty where there had been nothing. At the end of all this creating, God sized it all up, and pronounced that it was "very good." So, the first thing we can say of God's Word is that it is the agent of creation. Everything that is here; everything we can detect with the senses and a lot that we can't, is here because God called it to Be.

A second thing we can say about God's Word is that it is an agent of revelation. In fact we could say is it is God's revelation. Moses went up on the mountain to receive God's revelation. He received the Word of God -- the Law. And what a blessing that has been. "Blessed is the one whose delight is in the law of the Lord."

A third thing we can say about God's Word is that it is the source of Inspiration. The whole prophetic tradition hangs on this.

"The vision of Isaiah the son of Amoz, which he saw concerning Judah and Jerusalem in the days of Uzziah, Jotham, Ahaz, and Hezekiah, kings of Judah. Hear, O heavens, and give ear, O earth;

for the Lord has spoken.

". . . the word of the Lord came to Ezekiel the priest, the son of Buzi, in the land of the Chaldeans by the river Chebar; and the hand of the Lord was upon him there.

"The words of Amos, who was among the shepherds of Tekoa, which he saw concerning Israel in the days of Uzziah king of Judah and in the days of Joash, king of Israel, two years before the earthquake.

"Now the word of the Lord came to Jonah the son of Amittai, saying "Arise, go to Nineveh, that great city, and cry against it . ."

And so it goes, on and on and on through the prophetic tradition. And, some might say, right on up to the present times.

So, the word of God is creation, it is revelation, it is inspiration and, of course the whole Bible is commonly referred to as the Word of God. But there is at least one more specific reference to the Word we mustn't leave out: The prologue to John's gospel.

"In the beginning was the Word, and the Word was with God, and the Word was God. He was in the beginning with God; all things came into being through him, and without him not one thing came into being. In him was life, and the life was the light of all people. The light shines in the darkness, and the darkness has not overcome it . . . the true light, which enlightens everyone, was coming into the world.

"He was in the world, and the world came into being through him; yet the world did not know him. He came to what was his own, and his own people did not accept him. But to all who received him, who believed in his name, he gave power to become children of God, who were born, not of blood or of the will of men, but of God.

"And the word became flesh and lived among us, and we have seen his glory, the glory as of a father's only son, full of grace and truth . . . from his fullness we have received grace upon grace. The law indeed was given through Moses; grace and truth came through Jesus Christ.

Now, to sum up, I'll make one more point concerning the Word of God, and it's the point I pray, that stays with you the longest.

Whether we speak of Word as revelation or inspiration or incarnation; whether of law or prophets, or of the printed word or spoken word, it is a unity; it is ONE. In the beginning was the word and the word was with God, and the word was God. Think of it as you would the policy of a respected firm, or the word of a trusted friend. The Word and God are ONE. There is a unity there. And here is the clincher: When any of us stand up to preach, we are presuming to speak that word, the Word of God. God be with us. Amen!

ABOUT TIME

First Sermon Following Winter Break

I never had a digital watch, and, you know, I never wanted one. It's because of what they seem to say about the nature of time. A digital time piece doesn't give you a sense of the sweep of time-no sense of what went before; that might be worth remembering, or giving thanks for-or of what's out front, what to expect, or look foreword to, or hope for. Just that incessant shout of "now," "now," "now."

Hourglasses are tall. They make us quite conscious of the past; that's all that sand on the bottom; and of the future, that's the sand in the top. And they can be kind of discomforting, like when there is not much left in the top. But they do give us a sense of history. However, with hourglasses there is no "now," just grains of sand flitting through. And you can't reach in there to stop them.

Clocks are round. Looking at a clock is a little like looking at a map. You can see the past; that's where the hands have been. And you can see the future-where the hands are headed. In any given moment they are somewhat like the floor plan posted next to the elevator door with an arrow and a little note that says "you are here." However they seem to be saying that time is cyclical; round and round we go like a merry-go-round. But not really going anywhere.

So, hourglasses say there is no now. Digitals say there is nothing but now. Clocks say it doesn't really matter; it'll all come back around anyway.

Well, Happy New Year. We are now in Ought Five. And it is that time of the year when I have to take a little time to ponder the nature of time. St. Augustine said, "When I'm not thinking of time, I know what time is, but when I start think-

ing about time, I have no idea what it is." I have that problem
too. St Augustine believed that time, like stars and planets
and rocks and trees, was part of what God created. That was
his way of dealing with that old question: "What was God doing before he created everything?" Because, you see, if time
is part of what was created, there wasn't any "before." The
question makes no sense.

We tend to think of time and space as "givens." Space-time
is the context within which creation takes place. Augustine,
great theologian that he was, figured out theologically, that
time was at least was part of what was created. Centuries later
a great physicist figured that out scientifically. It was Albert
Einstein, in the last century, who showed that time is not absolute. It is relative to motion. The only absolute in creation
is the speed of light; 186,000 miles per second, regardless of
where the observer is or how the observer is moving.

Many ancient cultures had a cyclical view of time. Day follows day–seasons come in order, then repeat; generation follows generation. In some religions this cyclical view of things
carries over to people-reincarnation. In reincarnation, whether
one is rich or poor, sickly or strong, whatever one's fortune, depends on how well one lived out his previous incarnation. Our
current status is what we earned; it is what we deserve. So,
in such religions they speak of "compassion" not of "agape,"
Christian love. In compassion there is some sense of caring,
but it stops short of any compulsion to change anyone's plight.
That would be interfering with destiny. The poor soul is getting
exactly what is deserved. With agape (Christian love) there is
every compulsion to move into someone else's misfortune in an
attempt to help out; to change things.

It is quite difficult for us today to realize how revolutionary
the Hebrew sense of time was in those ancient times. In the
midst of many cultures who took it for granted that time is a
series of repeating cycles-clock time-there arose a people who
received the revelation that time is linear. Time had a beginning and time would have an end. With that kind of thinking
there comes a sense of history and with a sense of history,

a sense of meaning. Time seems to be going somewhere, so there must be meaning and purpose in there somehow. With a cyclical view of time there is no meaning; everything just keeps repeating. And with that perspective God is a god of place; as in a sacred mountain or tree.

Some of this crept into Hebrew thinking with their idea of a holy mountain and such, but it was doomed to die out. With a linier view of time and a sense of history and meaning, God is the God of history-a dynamic God. And it is God's agenda that is driving things. This brought a new perspective into play; a role reversal. If it's God's agenda, it's not my place to attempt to manipulate God in pursuit of my program; as the pagans did. It is my place to discern God's program and align myself with that. This was revolutionary thinking at the time, and those revelations are part of our heritage.

So, here we are, the beginning of a new year. We have memories of the past and we have hope for the future, but what about that elusive "now?" If there is no "now" how can I claim to "be?" What does it mean "to be" if there is no now?

Well, to me, those questions make sense logically, but they don't square with my experience. For me, there are certain "moments" in time that sort of "click" in a kind of "ah ha" experience. And with those "clicks" something else kicks into gear. Meaning radiates throughout my whole time line, traverses my history. Because of those clicks, lights go up and I see stuff in that new light. I see things in my past in that new light. And the new meaning shines forward adding new dimensions to my hopes and expectations. My whole history seems to have been following a plan I was not aware of along the way. Because of those clicks, that elusive and shadowy "now" is brilliantly lighted in every detail, revealing a totally awesome lifespan. The click might be a new insight that comes in a flash yet shines throughout my life. It might be the moment I experience forgiveness for someone who has wronged me. It might be a conversion experience which some people speak of as being born again. All of those have hit me from time to time, and I know they have hit you too.

In Greek there are two words we commonly translate into the English word "time." First there is "chronos." Chronos is clock time; time that goes on and on with no beginning or end. It just goes round and round in circles with no "now" and thus with no meaning. Time, as we usually think of time, or as Augustine would say "my understanding of time when I'm not thinking of time." Then there is "kairos." Kairos is THE time, or the critical time, or the right time. Or, as we might say, "It was timely." Chronos is my time line that can go on and on and on with little or no meaning. Kairos is that series of clicks that intervene from time to time bringing me brilliant new insights or filling my life with rich blessings till my heart overflows with love and gratitude.

In Christian Scripture chronos is assumed. But when they speak of the Christ event the word used is kairos. "In the fullness of time." At the right time; at the critical time, God sent his son. Eternity burst into history. The sense of the claim is that in the whole of human history, the Christ event is the center of time, fulfilling all that went before and interpreting all that follows. The Christ event fills history with meaning. The Christ event is THE KAIROS. But the Christ event transcends time. In Christ there is no chronos, only kairos. What this means is that all those "clicks" that hit you and me along the way, filling our lives with rich meaning, all of them are part of, all of them are manifestations, of THE kairos. The same kairos.

As existing beings we are separated, in chronos, from the Christ event by 2000 years. But in kairos we are right there with the whole company of heaven, right there with John and James and Paul, with Mary and Martha, right there at the birth, at the crucifixion, at the resurrection, totally present "in Christ." Now these "clicks" I speak of are experienced differently in different people. Some folk can report the precise time and place when they were born again, like Paul on the road to Damascus. Others, me included, will speak of multiple kairos experiences having a cumulative effect over time. I can indeed speak of one experience in particular that had an especially powerful effect on me. It came in the form of theological insight and it was dazzling and far reaching and I'll never forget it. I was in my study when it hit like a sledge hammer. Lights went on all over the place. I was dazed, stunned. I just sat there exploring my life's experiences for–I don't know how long. I wanted to examine everything in the light of this new revelation. Well, there have been others. In any case, the beginning of the year is a good time to think on such things.

Just how we "live in Christ" takes place on our journey in chronos, but it gets filled and fulfilled in kairos. And when kairos hits, we know we have entered into the salvation of our Lord.

DAILY BREAD

Grandfather's Magic Motorcycle

I'm sure you've noticed how a word or phrase that is very familiar to you suddenly jumps out and smacks you. All the other words fall into the background. But this one has you and you have to give it some attention. Well, this is a story of how that happened in church one day to a little boy.

It seems that a certain grandfather was in the habit of taking his grandson with him on his frequent errands around town. This included church on Sundays. The two were very close. Jimmy was about five as our story picks up, and it is Sunday morning. The lad sensed the deep devotion in the heart of the old man, so he went along with this weekly ritual so as not to give offence. He dutifully recited the words and went through the motions, but not much rubbed off on him.

That is, until one Sunday, during the Lord's Prayer, something struck the child. Excitedly, but very discreetly, he tugged on his grandfather's sweater sleeve. "Grandpa," he whispered, "What is dailybread? I know what French bread is, and wheat bread, and sour dough bread, but what's dailybread?"

"Dailybread," whispered the old man, "is what everybody needs to be truly alive."

The boy persisted, "Grandpa, You told me what dailybread does; what I want to know is what is it?

 "Later," promised the grandfather. It seemed like a long time to the child, as they went foreword to the altar, then back to their seats and yet another hymn to sing. Then there were greetings all around, the usual cup of apple juice and cookie. Finally, the two, now alone, sat down on a bench outside the church. "Now, I have this friend," explained Grandpa, "who has a magic motorcycle. I'll see if I can borrow it for this week, then we can take some trips together and maybe we can discover what daily-bread is."

"Wow" exclaimed Jimmy, "A motorcycle."

(Genesis 14: Peace)

The next day the two mounted the magic motorcycle and started down the interstate. When they got up to a reasonable speed, the motorcycle simply took off, like it had wings. Grandfather explained to the lad that they would visit a land far away and centuries back in history. (I know this sounds impossible, but for a magic motorcycle, it can be a one day trip.) Grandfather went on to explain that they would be present for the meeting of two very important people; Abram and King Melchizedek. Of course the boy didn't know who these people were. So Grandfather explained. Abram was the prince of a very large tribe of nomads, that is, people who lived in tents and moved around the country as needed to find pasture for their flocks. Abram had lots of servants and sheep and camels. Abram's nephew Lot also lived in the area and he too had lots of servants and flocks. This was a fairly wealthy and powerful family. Now, Melchizedek was King of Salem, a city built on a hill which would one day be called Jerusalem. Melchizedek was also priest of God Most High, so he could bless people and stuff like that.

There were also many little kingdoms in the area and they were constantly at war with one another. They would raid each other's camps stealing and looting, killing off the men, capturing the slaves and flocks, and there seemed no end to it. Abram, tried to keep out of it. Then one day several of those kings got together and ganged up on one major city. It just happened that Lot and his family and servants and flocks and everything he had were there at the time and they were all captured. When Abram heard about it he said, "Well, that's the last straw."

So he rounded up his men and went over there and beat the tar out of the whole bunch. And he freed Lot and his people. "Now", continued Grandpa, "We are arriving at Abram's camp just as he returns from the rescue of Lot and his victory over those renegade kings, and just as King Melchizedek comes down to meet Abram." So, the two of them watch quietly as these two powerful rulers greet each other. Then King Melchizedek gives

Abram a loaf of bread, and then he blesses him.

"Why", queried Grandfather, "do you suppose that the priest of God Most High gave Abram the bread?"

"Well," the lad responded thoughtfully, "Abram is a very powerful man; I think that the king wants peace with Abram. And since Abram took the bread, that must mean that Abram wants peace too. . . . Say Grandpa, was that dailybread?"

"Well, I said that dailybread is what everyone needs to be truly alive; what do you think?"

(Exodus 16: Gifts)

Next day the two were up at the crack of dawn, got on the magic motorcycle and started down the interstate once more. Again, Grandfather explained where they were going, this time to visit Moses and the children of Israel in the wilderness. As they traveled, Grandfather provided a little background on Moses and the king of Egypt, about the escape of the Israelite slaves and the crossing of the Red Sea. And he explained what a rebellious and stiff necked-people the children of Israel were. Even though the Lord had rescued them from slavery under the Egyptians, they did nothing but complain. In due course the children of Israel found themselves deep in the wilderness with nothing to eat. So God sent manna from heaven.

Now nobody knew what manna was. In the Hebrew language the word means "What is it?" which is not much help. Anyway God did give them some strict instructions. Every morning the men were to gather just enough manna to feed their families for that day. No more–no less. And they were not supposed to keep it overnight. After the morning gathering and feeding the left-over manna simply evaporated. But next morning, there it was all fresh and new again. However, this was indeed a stiff-necked, rebellious people. So, it would take some convincing. Anyway, grandfather and grandson landed in the wilderness just in time to see the morning gathering. As they watched, they observed some of the men greedily gathering more than they needed. But when they got to their tents to feed their families they discovered that they had no extra after all. Then some other greedy fellows tried to hide some of the manna for next day, in case they should run short. But the next day they found that the hoarded manna was full of worms.

"Well" asked Grandfather, "What do you make of the manna?"

"I suppose," responded Jimmy, "You could call that daily-bread, but you said dailybread is what everybody needs to be truly alive. These people are all messed up; I wouldn't call that truly alive. I think," He continued, "that manna is a reminder from God that all gifts are from God, and we don't have to be greedy or selfish; just be grateful for today's gifts and let tomorrow take care of itself."

(Mark 6: The Picnic)

The next day Grandfather had some errands he had to cover. So they parked the bike and took the old pick-up. Of course Jimmy tagged along. They went to the market, then to the hardware store and a couple of other places. Then it was Thursday and they were off again on their adventure, once more flying down the interstate on the magic motorcycle. This time, Grandfather explained, they would visit Jesus on an isolated hillside where some 5000 people had gathered to hear him preach and maybe, see him work some miracles. The lad already knew the story so grandfather didn't have a lot of explaining to do.

When they got there it was evening. The people were getting restless as they had not had anything to eat all day. Furthermore, they were a long way from any of the villages. The disciples were urging Jesus to send the crowd on their way so they could find some food. But Jesus said, "You give them something to eat."

But, they responded, "We've looked high and low and all we can come up with is a little bit of bread and these two fish."

"Well, make them sit down and we'll feed them," The two watched expectantly as Jesus blessed the food and began to break it up for the distribution. He passed it out to the disciples and motioned for them to get with it. The disciples started to break up the food and pass it along. And the more they broke it up and passed it out, the more they had. After a little while all 5000 had eaten their fill and they still had twelve baskets of bread left over.

"So, what do you make of that?" asked Grandfather.

"Wow," exclaimed the boy, "It's just like the children of Israel in the wilderness and the manna from heaven. God surely does love his people; he can use Moses in the wilderness or Jesus on the hillside to feed them. I suppose that means he could use us too. But that's still ordinary people and ordinary bread. You said that dailybread is what everyone needs to be truly alive. I still don't know what dailybread is."

(Mark 14: Remembering)

On Friday, Grandfather once again picked up Jimmy for their travel adventure. This time, Grandfather explained, they would be silent and invisible guests at Jesus' and his disciples' final meal together. They arrived just as Jesus and his group were entering the inn where they had reserved a large room upstairs for their dinner. They all took their places. There was some initial confusion over who would be the betrayer. Then they settled into the meal which Jesus blessed. He called the bread his body and the wine his blood. Then he shared it all with them, and he told them, "From now on whenever you share the bread and the wine, remember me, and I'll be there with you."

Later, as the two reflected on the experience, Jimmy mused (barely out loud) "Hey, that 'remember me' part is a lot like what we do on Sunday, isn't it Grandpa?" Then, "That must be why we go to church, to remember."

Finally it was Sunday. As the two came to church the child reflected on the week's adventures: "You know, dailybread means peace, and it means gifts from God, and it means love and it has something to do with being together and sharing–but I still don't know what it is!"

Soon they were in church, singing the old familiar hymns; someone read the lessons, then the offering, then the Great Thanksgiving and the Lord's Prayer. And that word again, "Dailybread."

"Dailybread is what everybody needs to be truly alive" thought Jimmy. Then the two went to the altar rail. Suddenly something 'clicked' inside the boy's head, again he grabbed Grandfather's sweater sleeve, "Grandpa, I know what dailybread is–dailybread is Jesus–what everybody needs to be truly alive"

Just then the Eucharistic Minister pressed a morsel of bread into the palm of Jimmy's hand, "The Body of Christ," then on to

Grandfather. The two looked at each other. Jimmy smiled, Grandfather winked, then spontaneously and together they mouthed the words of the prayer, "Give us today our dailybread."

GOD SHOWS NO PARTIALITY

Easter 2005

Then Peter began to speak to them; "I truly understand that God shows no partiality, but in every nation anyone who fears him and does what is right is acceptable to him."

What we have here-in this brief reading from the Book of Acts-is a glimpse of very early Christian preaching. Peter's sermon can be outlined in three parts: First the introduction, "I truly understand that God shows no partiality," and he goes on to note that every nation has its share of people of faith. The main body of the sermon is the story of Jesus-about as compact as you could get it-from his baptism through his resurrection. He then closes with the notation that all the prophets had testified about him, that anyone who believed would receive salvation. But here is a question: "To whom is this sermon preached?"

The sermon is one short paragraph out of the tenth chapter of the Book of Acts. So let's take a look at the context. As the chapter opens we are introduced to a certain Roman centurion named Cornelius stationed at the port city of Caesarea on the Palestinian coast. Cornelius, we are told, was a devout man who feared God and he and his whole household, steadfast in their prayers and generous in their alms giving.

The story begins one afternoon when Cornelius, deep into his regular 3:00 prayers, slips into a trance and experiences a vision of an angel of God. The angel tells Cornelius to send for a man called Peter who was, at that time staying at a certain house in Joppa-another port city some thirty miles to the south. So Cornelius calls in three of his trusted people, explains all this to them and sends them off to Joppa, a walk that would take about a day and a half. When they get to Joppa they find Peter and convince him to join them. So, Peter and a few other Christians of Joppa hike back on up to Cornelius' house in Caesarea. Then Cornelius gathers his household together, family, slaves, probably some of the soldiers assigned to him to hear what Peter has to say, and this is a brief account of Peter's sermon, preached to Cornelius' household–because they were eager to hear.

But the story is actually a little more complicated than that. You see, while Cornelius' messengers were on their way south to Joppa, the second day out, Peter had gone up on the roof of the house for noonday prayers. Now, having skipped lunch that day, Peter was praying on an empty stomach. Anyway, he sort of slipped into dreamland and he saw a vision. In this vision something like a big net descended from heaven with all kinds of animals, foul, and crawly things on it, and a voice said, "Get up Peter–kill and eat!"

Now, we have to remember that Peter was a devout Jew who could only eat kosher food and he was incredibly offended by this order. "I can't eat that stuff; it's profane and unclean." And the voice said, "What God calls clean you shall not call profane." This whole scene was repeated three times and just about jarred Peter out of his sandals. What could it possibly mean? Then came a knock on the door. And Peter, still outraged by the very idea and puzzling over the meaning of such a vision, went downstairs to meet Cornelius' messengers. Now what in the world could these Gentiles possibly want with a Jew? However, with his mind going round in circles and his head not quite screwed on straight, he opened the house to these strangers and provided hospitality.

The next day they all set out for Caesarea and as they walked, Peter's vision gradually began to sink in. In due course they find themselves before Cornelius' assembly when Peter stands to speak and the revelation finally connects and explodes: "I truly understand–yes, I really, really do get it. God shows no partiality. Even people like you–Italians and Greeks–every nation has its faithful people. See, I really did get it."

Then, at the end of the sermon, like he's trying to make sure that he doesn't lose it – "Yes, all the prophets testified of him: that everyone who believes, everyone, receives salvation. All

God's creation is holy and we are not to call any of it unclean."

Seen this way, Peter's sermon, at least part of it, was addressed to Peter. The new insight had to be said out loud–to make sure it stuck.

Well, actually, there is still another way to hear this story. The Book of Acts was written by someone traditionally called Luke who also wrote the Gospel of that name. And we can assume that it was written for some Christian community Luke was associated with. Chapter 10 recounts the tale of a hardheaded, narrow minded and prejudiced Jew, the first of the apostles, who was repeatedly clobbered by God and dragged into an experience that would turn him around 180 degrees; but one step at a time. (Some people take a lot of convincing.)

The first step: A dazed and disoriented Peter opens the house to those Gentile messengers. Second step: Hardly knowing why, he agrees to go with them to Caesarea. There were many steps along that road, and we can assume, a lot of talk as those people tried to understand each other and what God was doing with them. Peter's sermon was the next step. And then–as though to nail down the message once and for all, there is another stunning episode reported in the final paragraph of Chapter 10.

While Peter was still preaching there was a great Wooosh and Zapp and the Holy Spirit descended on all Cornelius' people. Peter and his friends from Joppa stood there dumbfounded as Cornelius and his whole household danced around, glorified God, praised Jesus, jabbered in tongues, and in general acted like a bunch of people just off a Cursillo weekend. It was a second Pentecost, only this time a Gentile Pentecost. Peter and his gang looked at each other, "Why, the Holy Spirit has come upon them just as she did with us." Then Peter shrugged, "So, what's to prevent them from being baptized? Go get the water." And they baptized the whole household in the name of Christ Jesus.

Seen this way, the message is addressed to Luke's household of faith who were probably as hard-headed, narrow-minded and prejudiced as Peter, and their message is something like this: "Look, we are Jew and Gentile, Arab and Greek, black and white, we are simple and wise, and there are lots of differences, but in Christ we are one."

Out of Scripture such as this we get our Baptismal Covenant; "Will you seek and serve Christ in all persons and respect the dignity of every human being?"

When Lynne and I were in private practice in Colorado we used to frequent a certain conference center in Nevada. It was run by an Anglican order of nuns, The Sisters of Charity. Sister Faith, who was in charge of the place, had a special warm spot for Lynne and me, making sure that we got favored treatment when possible. One time as we arrived for a meeting she sought me out and called out, "Oh Chuck, I have to tell you a story." It seems that she had been leading a local study group and the story came out of the experience of a woman in this group.

The woman had gone to one of those small convenience stores to pick up something. As she crossed the parking lot, heading for the entrance, she was approached by a shabbily dressed man of the streets, who clearly wanted something. He was holding on to some kind of rag draped over one arm. "Pardon me, mam, could you please . . ."

She clutched her purse, avoided his eyes, and hurried into the shop. Later, while waiting at the check out stand, she could see him in the parking lot, still soliciting. Another woman passed him by. The clerk went out to shoo him away from the shop door, but he didn't leave the lot. Finally it was time for the woman to return to her car. Making sure she had a firm grip on her belongings, she started for the parking lot. Sure enough the man approached again, still with the cloth draped over one arm. "Pardon me, mam, could you please . . .

But this time something made her hear him out, "Could you please help me with this bandage; I just can't hold it together to get it started, once started I'll be just fine." She looked and saw a badly mangled wrist; of course he couldn't get the bandage started with one hand. She turned her attention to the injured arm and helped him get the cloth in place. Once it was firmly anchored, he was able to take care of it. Finally, and for the first time, the woman looked up into the man's face. It was the face of Christ.

Seen this way, Peter's sermon is addressed to us.

Easter Blessings All
From Lynne and Chuck

OUTRAGEOUS, IRREVERENT, JOYFUL

Marks of a Bold Christian

Bishop Daniel Corrigan was surely one of the most outrageous, irreverent and joyful Christians I've ever known. I take all those to be positive qualities by the way. I'll explain in a minute. Dan Corrigan was Suffragan Bishop of Colorado in the late 50's. In 1960 he was called to one of three key positions in the Episcopal Church Center in New York City; head of the Home Department. In 1966 I was called as an appointed officer of our National Church staff and when I got to New York, discovered that I would be in the bishop's chain of command. Dan Corrigan was my boss, two levels up.

Tumultuous times–the late 60's. The cities were burning. Every university, every national church, most other institutions were under attack; crisis everywhere. One by one the national churches went through a "restructuring," a futile rearranging of the deck chairs, until it became a joke. This was also the period that saw two new fashions spread like wildfire throughout the world: the mini-skirt and the bikini. I once heard Dan Corrigan remark to someone regarding the bikini, "Well, what they reveal is interesting, but what they conceal is essential."

When a new ecumenical seminary was formed in Rochester, N.Y. involving several denominations working together, it marked a significant ecumenical breakthrough and Dan was a most enthusiastic supporter. Commenting on the intimate relationships of all these groups working together under one roof, before a rather large ecumenical assembly, Dan off-handedly remarked, "Now this is face to face ecumenicity . . . and everybody knows that if you are going to get into bed with someone, face to face is the only way to go."

I recall a big meeting in Chicago one time involving maybe 20 people representing our national church staff and elected council members plus our counterparts from the Presbyterian and United (UCC) churches. While we were meeting, a big blow up occurred in Washington DC throwing the then brand new poverty program (which we all supported) into crisis. A tactic was quickly devised to strengthen Sargent Shiver's hand (who was taking the brunt of the attack because of funding a child development program in Mississippi) by flying to Washington and joining a demonstration already under way. We would lease a plane to fly all sixty or so of us. Of course, we knew what this would do to newspaper headlines all over the nation; key officials of three main-line churches demonstrating in DC.

Jack Woodard, my immediate boss, thought he'd better phone Dan to give him a "heads up" and a chance to veto the plan. He did–and went to great lengths to explain what we were about. Dan listened patiently and when Jack finally finished, drawled, "Well, sounds ok for starters!" Dan was, incidentally, one of the bishops involved in the illegal ordination of the "Philadelphia Eleven" (Women ordained before it was canonically permitted).

I once heard Dan preach before a large ecumenical caucus. He stood in the open, no notes, and kept us all spell bound as he held forth on the subject of change. Then, on the Exodus, he noted that Moses was just helping the Egyptians with their re-structuring. Later as they crossed the Red Sea he quoted Moses by noting "My children, we are, you might say, living in an age in transition." On another occasion he was presiding at the Eucharist in the open, in a city park. There was a pond nearby with wild geese paddling around. As it came time for the distribution, three or four of the curious geese came waddling up to the assembly straining their necks to see what was going on. Without missing a beat and with a grin on his face, Dan met the geese with the tray of wafers and continued down the line "Body of Christ, "body of Christ."

So, maybe that will illustrate what I mean by outrageous, ir-reverent and joyful. But I'll take it a step further. The opposite of outrageous as I mean it here, is "predictable." By irreverent I mean free–free of entanglements in all the rules and regulations. So the opposite of irreverent is something like obedient to the letter-all bound up. The opposite of joyful is, obviously, sad. I can't recall Dan not seeing the humor in anything. So, you see, a Christian who is outrageous, irreverent and joyful is likely to be boldly creative and is certainly fun to be around. One who is predictable, obedient and sad is-well-dull, and a bore to be around.

Now, my reason for profiling Dan Corrigan is that I see Philip as a first century Corrigan-or-maybe, Dan as a 20th century Philip. But before we get further into that let's take a look at that other character from today's reading.

The Ethiopian eunuch is indeed an interesting character. First of all he was a high ranking official reporting directly to the queen and he was in charge of her entire treasure. In some cultures, in some periods of history, castrating young boys was as common as it is with young bulls here in Wyoming. It's a lot easier to raise steers than bulls. So, to assure that your male servants would be docile and faithful, castration might be the way to go. Of course a eunuch, having never experienced his maleness, never knew what he was missing, so tended to settle down and make the most of his lot in life. In some cases, as with our Ethiopian, he might rise to considerable heights of responsibility.

A second thing we can take note of here is that our Ethiopian was a "God fearer." This means that he was drawn to the Hebrew faith; he followed the faith as far as he could. However, he could never be a full member of the household of faith in Jewish tradition (never mind his high-ranking at home) because in Jewish eyes he was only half a man. Now, Ethiopia was an African nation in the upper reaches of the Nile, which probably means that this man was black. Now, get this, this guy came all the way from the upper Nile to Jerusalem on some kind of pilgrimage, "to worship in Jerusalem," we are told, and is now returning to his homeland when he encounters Philip.

He may be a high ranking court official at home but among Jews he is a black man, a foreigner, a eunuch-definitely an outsider. And Philip is, of course, Jewish. When the Spirit; (the primary hero in the Book of Acts, and, we should note, traditionally a feminine figure) . . . when the Spirit prompts Philip, (who knows the law, the tradition and the prejudices) to join the eunuch in his chariot, he jumps at the chance and patiently and thoroughly teaches him the Good News beginning with the passage from Isaiah which the man had been reading, right on up to the Easter experience. Then, they come to that pool of water. Can you see the questions, the doubts, the fear written all over the face of that guy? He too knows the rules. "Look, water, what's to prevent me from being baptized?"

Well, as we've seen, all kinds of traditions and rules are right there, blocking. There's plenty in the way of his baptism. A more timid soul might be inclined to mutter something like, "well, I don't know, I better go check this out with Peter." But no, not Philip. Philip, you recall is our first century Christian who is outrageous, irreverent and joyful. So he grabs that fellow by the hand and the two run down that bank, splash into the water until they are about waist deep, Philip dunks him three times, says some words, and that eunuch emerges a member of Christ, a child of God, and an inheritor of the Kingdom of Heaven. DONE! And one more is added to the ranks of the Christians, for, we are told, that Ethiopian went on his way rejoicing.

My sisters and brothers, we face some grave issues in the life of the church today, and sometimes we might feel a bit rattled by them. But there's no shortage of bold witnesses from Philip in the first century to Corrigan in the sixties, from the devout women who gathered at the tomb to this gathering here today. Christians of all times who are all part of the great cloud of witnesses and who dare to be outrageous, irreverent and joyful. But, just to remind you once more, bottom line, it's not up to us; the real hero in the Book of Acts is the Holy Spirit. So I can tell you what happened when Philip finally did get back to Peter after that irregular baptism. He shrugged and explained, "Well, she made me do it!"

September 26, 2004   Proper 19 (A) Eccl.27:30-28:7, Psm.103:8-13,
Rom.14, Matt.18:21-3521

SEVENTY SEVEN TIMES

Forgiving One Another

I was trying to remember the words of a song. (I can recall the
tune). Maybe it's from a musical? Maybe you can help?

> You always hurt the one you love
> The one you wouldn't hurt at all.
> You always take the sweetest rose
> And crush it till the petals fall . . . .

. . . then I lose it . . . However the last two lines of
that first stanza are:

> So if I broke your heart last night
> It's because I love you most of all.

There is one simple way to avoid hurting someone or being
hurt: don't get that close. That's what makes us vulnerable.
Don't fall in love; put on a thick skin, don't get involved, stay out
of it. If you just don't care-then you are not vulnerable, nobody
can touch you!

. . . . But, then you are . . . alone.

Our readings this afternoon – all of them – are about community. Not alone-ness, but togetherness; therefore about loving
one another, or, we might say, about remaining vulnerable; risking getting hurt and risking hurting someone. And the message
in those readings-all of them-is that the real stuff of community
maintenance is forgiveness-at least that's the first part.

Now there is nothing in here to imply that we are to be wishy-
washy or casual about sin-about behavior or about standards. It is
not suggesting that offenses are not serious or pain real. The pain
can be very serious. And the deeper the love, the more we are at
risk of hurting or of being hurt.

The second part of the message is that we forgive because we
are forgiven. Actually, it's stronger than that. We must forgive

if we are to experience forgiveness. And it's not just a recipro-
cal arrangement, as between two people; you forgive me and I'll
forgive you-although that's part of it. It's much bigger than that.
It's that God-Being Itself-the eternal I AM-has forgiven me. Who
in the world am I then, not to forgive?

Hear this from the Book of Ecclesiasticus:

"Anger and wrath, these also are abominations, yet a sinner
holds on to them. The vengeful will face the Lord's vengeance,
for he keeps a strict account of their sins. Forgive your neighbor
the wrong he has done, and then your sins will be pardoned when
you pray. Does anyone harbor anger against another, and expect
healing from the Lord? If one has no mercy toward another like
himself, can he then seek pardon for his own sins?"

And this from Psalm 103:

"The Lord is full of compassion and mercy, slow to anger and
of great kindness.He will not always accuse us, nor will he keep
his anger forever. He has not dealt with us according to our sins.
nor rewarded us according to our wickedness. For as the heavens
are high above the earth, so is his mercy great upon those who
fear him.

As far as the east is from the west, so far has he removed our
sins from us. As a father cares for his children, so does the Lord
care for those who fear him."

And this from Paul's letter to the Romans

"Why do you pass judgment on your brother or sister? Or you,
why do you despise your brother or sister? For we all stand before
the judgment seat of God."

And finally, this from today's Gospel:

"Peter came and said to Jesus, "Lord, if another member of
the church sins against me, how often should I forgive? As many
as seven times?" Jesus said to him, "Not seven times, but, I tell
you, seventy-seven times. For this reason the kingdom of heaven
may be compared to a king who wished to settle accounts with
his slaves. When he began the reckoning, one who owed him ten
thousand talents was brought to him; and as he could not pay, his
lord ordered him to be sold, together with his wife and children
and all his possessions, and payment to be made. So the slave fell
on his knees before him, saying, 'Have patience with me, and I

will pay you everything.' And out of pity for him, the lord of that slave released him and forgave him the debt.

But that same slave, as he went out, came upon one of his fellow slaves who owed him a hundred denarii; and seizing him by the throat, he said, 'Pay what you owe.' Then his fellow slave fell down and pleaded with him, 'Have patience with me, and I will pay you.' But he refused; then he went and threw him into prison until he would pay the debt. When his fellow slaves saw what had happened, they were greatly distressed, and they went and reported to their lord all that had taken place. Then his lord summoned him and said to him, 'You wicked slave! I forgave you all that debt because you pleaded with me Should you not have had mercy on your fellow slave, as I had mercy on you?' And in anger his lord handed him over to be tortured until he would pay his entire debt. So my heavenly Father will also do to everyone of you, if you do not forgive your brother or sister from your heart."

The parable is loaded with outrageous exaggerations. Consider these:

How could a slave incur a debt of two or three million dollars? What's the point of selling him into slavery when he already is a slave? In any case, how would he then be able to pay? And torturing the poor fellow will not help matters. Regarding the second slave, what's the point of throwing him into prison "until he pays?"

Gross exaggerations -- the story teller's license. Yet that is precisely the point. The forgiveness we might be inclined to grant one another is like pennies compared with the awesome graciousness we experience under a Lord who has removed our sins from us "as far as the east is from the west. For as the heavens are high above the earth, so is his mercy great upon those who fear him." Considering this abundance of grace how dare we not forgive one another?

Over the summer I've been studying ahead in preparation for the preaching this fall. One of the passages that caught my attention was Jesus' parable of the king who wanted to give a wedding feast for his son. It was to be a real bash-the party of the year. So he makes his preparations, then sends his servants out to hand deliver the invitations to the chosen list. But it seems that all the big-wigs invited have some lame duck excuse for offering their regrets. So, the king, undaunted, sends his servants out into the city, the slums, the alleys to invite everyone to the feast. We are going, by damn, to have a party any way. The banquet hall is filled.

The king decides to go out and mingle with the guests, and as he does, he singles out one guest in particular and says "Friend, how did you get in here without a wedding gown?" The poor guest was speechless, so the king has him thrown out. Now this is a very strange twist in the story. The hall is filled with street people: beggars, bag ladies, tramps, harlots, you name it; what does the king expect to see, tuxedos and long formal gowns?

One of my resources in studying this stuff is a set of books by Robert Farrar Capon on the parables. Capon doesn't miss the irony in this twist so he spins a yarn about how the wedding feast becomes a costume party with the king supplying the duds out of the royal wardrobe. The point that he picks up on is the notation that "the guest was speechless." The king was prepared to accept everybody, regardless of their station in life. In fact he already has accepted everybody; just look around the hall and see. The guest could have said anything and be OK with the king. But "he was speechless." Capon's point is that we find it terribly difficult to accept the fact that God accepts us regardless of who we are or what we've done. Capon fantasizes on the conversations that might have taken place between the king and the guest without a wedding gown:

Guest: "If he thinks I'm going to put on an unfitted tuxedo and hobnob with all those deadbeats . . .

King: "Oh, just shut up, will you, and have a drink on the house.

Guest: "Hey! I want to be recognized for myself, not just accepted because somebody put a monkey suit on me.

King: "Dummy! The monkey suits are just for fun; it's the people in them I went to the bother of dragging here. Try the caviar; it's real Beluga.

Guest: "Maybe if I say nothing and just look dumb, he won't notice how poorly I'm dressed.

King: "Turkey! You actually think that I invited all these losers because they passed some kind of test? Relax; this whole party is free.

So, (Capon's point) the guest could have said anything and be home free with the king; but, "he was speechless."

I remember when my two older children were in the first and second grades (I was in seminary). The younger, Bill, had a bad habit of scribbling on any scrap of paper he happened upon. He had been scolded many times for the offence, so he knew better, but he still did it. The older, Charlene, had some considerable artistic talent and she was meticulous and persistent, and her creations involved a lot of careful attention to detail.

On this one occasion, (I just happened to be around the corner from the open door) Charlene discovered her latest work of fine art covered with scribbling. Enraged, she tore into Bill and read him the riot act at the top of her lungs. I decided to stay out of it and see how they would work it out. So, I remained hidden and just listened. Well, Bill was guilty as sin and he knew it. Furthermore, he could see that he had inflicted a lot of pain in an act he was supposed to stay clear of. Instead of fighting back, with a heart full of remorse, he just sobbed. (I continued to stay out of it.) At that point it became clear to Charlene that she had over-reacted and had caused way too much damage. The room became curiously quiet. After a minute or so of silence, I cautiously peaked around the corner–and saw two kids in a full embrace quietly crying on one another's shoulders. There was a barely audible whisper, "It's OK, Bill."

So it is with all of us. We only hurt the one we love.

And then we embrace . . . and healing comes,

And in that embrace, there is joy in heaven.

BUT IT'S JUST NOT FAIR

Justice and Grace

Nearly 1700 years ago-around the year 325 CE-a distinguished and highly esteemed Jewish scholar died unexpectedly and at a very tender age; Rabbi Bunn bar Hijia. In fact, it is said that he died on the very day his only son was born. His son, named for his father would come to be known as Rabbi Bunn II. "It just wasn't fair." So it would seem to members of this distraught family. And, probably someone voiced this sense of betrayal. You live according to the rules; you expect just treatment. Things are supposed to be fair. Jews are steeped in the law. The prophets hammered them with principals of justice. They knew the meaning of fair. And here was one of their most promising leaders, a brand new father, dead at such a young age. His colleagues, who had been his teachers, planned and conducted the funeral, selecting one of their own to preach. The preacher began his homily with a parable.

There was a certain king who, at harvest time, rounded up a crew of laborers, came to agreement with them concerning a day's wage and sent them into the vineyard. The king strolled up and down along the edge of the field, keeping an eye on things as the work commenced. About an hour or so into the day the king called one of the workers over to him and struck up a conversation as they both walked up and down along the side of the vineyard. The day wore on and the laborer who had been singled out never did get back into the field, causing some minor griping among the other workers-one of their fellows wasn't pulling his share. At the end of the day the king called his steward and arranged for the payment of the laborers. Each man received the standard pay for a day's work, including the man who had barely worked an hour. With this the grumbling greatly intensified until it came to the attention of the king. The king called the workers together.

"I've been told that some of you don't think I'm being fair in the matter of your pay. First of all, let me point out that you received the amount that we agreed to. That's fair, is it not? If you are miffed at the fact that I also paid one of you who had put in less than a day, at the same rate, I have two responses for you; first, it's my money, am I not allowed to use it as I see fit? Second, I spent the first part of the day closely observing your work. The man that I showed the favor to was as productive in one hour as were the rest of you working all day. He did indeed earn a full day's pay. You have no complaint."

You will recognize the similarity of the rabbi's parable with the one I just read from Jesus; not exactly the same but close enough to suspect that there was a common source. So, consider this, did the rabbi copy Jesus' original story with a little editorial work to make it suitable for his purposes? (By the year 325 Jesus' teachings would have been in circulation.) Or did they both work from an earlier common source? Scholars who study such questions would say that the story was Jesus' original. One of the clues is the way stories (not just fish stories) tend to grow with much telling; call it creeping exaggeration. Note that Jesus' story is about a landowner. In the Rabbi's story the landowner has become a king.

But still, that's a minor adjustment in detail. Any story teller has a right to add personal flourishes in retelling a story. That's understood and acceptable. This story teller however went a lot further than that. This story teller radically changed the whole point of the story. It really makes no difference on the impact of the story whether the subject is a landowner or a king. The point of the story will come across either way. But in this case we have a story teller who has modified the story to make it support his sense of justice. The story, as told by Jesus, would definitely not support this point. The rabbi-preacher was out to justify the life of the rabbi who died too young, and, we might note, before a congregation steeped in the same view of things.

He was under a compulsion to show that justice had not been thwarted. That compulsion is deeply rooted in the Jewish sense of justice. Justice is about balancing the books. It's about Law; about the prophetic tradition. Justice is about punishing the wrong-doer and rewarding the righteous. Justice is about being fair. And we are hard wired to know when things are not fair.

This rabbi-preacher was compelled to show somehow that, bottom line, justice was in fact served. In his version of the parable, the laborer who worked a mere one hour was so productive in that hour, he actually earned the full day's pay. (ergo: That the rabbi died so young does not mean that the promise of his life went unfulfilled.)

"But, it's just not fair!" We've heard those words from a small child with little experience and no apparent training in the subject. Where does it come from? Say, an accident, someone is killed, no obvious culprit, and the question is, "Why her?" Or, "Why him?" And the implied notation, "It just isn't fair!" Yes, we have an innate sense of what's fair. If our parable had been about laborers who had been promised a certain sum, then at the end of the day, were paid less, or nothing, we could yell out, "Hey, that's not fair!" And we'd have lots of company. But, in Jesus' story, most of the laborers were paid more. And still, all that complaining; it's still not perceived as fair. And, as we can see, in a kind of perverse way, it isn't.

But that brings us to the radical difference between the two parables: Jesus' parable of the landowner, and the rabbi's parable of the king. The rabbi's compulsion drives him to show that justice prevails even though that requires a huge change in the message. Jesus' parable is not about what's fair–it's about grace. As a matter of fact, it's about outrageous generosity. What employer could afford to throw money around as Jesus' landowner has? It's not economically responsible or even feasible. You just couldn't stay in business very long practicing that kind of stewardship. Maybe the guys retained at noon, at 3 o'clock, etc. had families to feed at the end of the day, and the landowner knew it. That might explain the generosity. But it's still not fair. And it does not account for how the landowner could afford such irresponsible management of his resources.

So, we have two world views here. In one, things are fair; or at least expected to be. If you put in a day's work, you deserve a reasonable day's wage. If you commit a crime, you can expect to be held to account for it. If your team wins the contest, your team gets the prize and the acclaim. It's the kind of world in which we would probably be moved to observe, "Well that's fair enough!" or, "that's what I call justice". This is the world of the rabbi-preacher. And it is not a bad world. And it is not a world we would reject on principal. If we could bring about this kind of world, there would be no reason for anyone to go around claiming, "But it's just not fair." In fact, if we could bring about this kind of world, it would be quite an accomplishment. What more could we ask for?

But it is not the world Jesus is preaching about. On the other hand Jesus' parable of the landowner should not sound all that strange on our ears. We already live in that world. But we sometimes forget. Lynne and I are what are commonly called "cradle Episcopalians." That is to say, we were born into the church, nurtured by the church, grew up in the church. As a matter of fact I could go on bragging, as Paul did, about my extensive family history in the Anglican Church. But, also like Paul, I would catch myself and admit that there really is no point or merit in such bragging. Because as we all know, one baptized into the faith yesterday is just as much a member of Christ, a child of God and an inheritor of the Kingdom of Heaven as any of us. We know that, and no one would ever catch us arguing to the contrary. So, we know that there is nothing in here to brag about, no matter our history, the one who is called and sent into the vineyard during the last hour is treated the same as the rest, not because it is fair, but because of the abundant grace of the one who calls.

So, we have two world views here. "The kingdom of heaven" Jesus says, "is like a landowner" who went out early, midday and late, to call workers into his harvest.

WHO? ME?

On Vocation

First sermon following a Saturday workshop on vocation (Epip.+5c) Workshop postponed

Some years ago, on a cross country flight, I had an aisle seat, left side, in the front of the cabin, and the plane was about one third full. I was working on a manuscript of some kind and I had my tray table down. The one for the unoccupied seat next to me was down also, and both tables strewn with papers, notes and a couple of reference books. I was fairly well boxed in. Then I decided that I wanted to look up a Biblical verse to reference in my paper, but I didn't have a Bible. I knew that planes usually carry a Bible in their assortment of reading material, and I could see a stack of magazines and stuff in the open overhead compartment across the aisle and a seat or two in front of me. I couldn't get up under the circumstances, so I hailed a cabin attendant. She responded quickly. I pointed to the open compartment and asked if she would check to see if there might be a Bible stashed in there with all the magazines. She ruffled through the stack, and I went on with what I was doing. She was back in a minute or so, looked at me very seriously and reported, "No sir, I didn't see one in there,"

I thanked her and went on with my task (I could look it up later). She didn't leave; she stood there for a moment, hesitantly, then got down on one knee, put her arm across my shoulder and asked, "Are you frightened sir?" (Why else would anyone want a Bible on a plane?) I assured her that I was OK and she went about her business. What I knew that she probably didn't was that the Gideons routinely place Bibles on commercial planes as they do in hotel and motel rooms. In my travel, I frequently take advantage of that. For one traveling light, every little bit helps.

Anyway, Gideon is one of my favorite Old Testament characters. I once saw Peter Ustinov play Gideon in a TV short stand up piece. He looked and sounded soooo pathetic. It was a fantastic performance, and a great experience of the character Gideon.

What I wanted to call to your attention was Gideon's response to God's call. The Israelites were a terribly put-down people. They were constantly bullied by the Midianites who sacked their grain, burned their fields and in general played havoc with them. So the Israelites were hiding out. In today's reading we are told that Gideon was beating out wheat (thrashing) in the wine press, (of all places) "to hide it from the Midianites." Now, in the midst of all this misery and hopelessness, an angel of the Lord appears to Gideon with this astounding greeting, "The Lord is with you, you mighty man of valor," Then, "Go in this might of yours, and deliver Israel from the hand of Midian; I hereby commission you."

Is this angel completely off his rocker, out of touch with reality? So Gideon replies "But sir, how can I deliver Israel? My clan is the weakest in Manasseh, and I am the least in my family."

In the second of today's readings we hear Paul recounting his call. It's a resurrection appearance of Jesus; Paul reports: "Last of all, he appeared also to me, for I am the least of apostles, unfit to be called an apostle."

Then in the Gospel, we hear Peter's response to Jesus' call, "Go away from me Lord, for I am a sinful man." And so it is when God's call comes to any of us. Recall the angel's visit to Mary, "Greetings, favored one. The Lord is with you." But Mary, we are told, "was much perplexed by his words and pondered what sort of greeting this might be."

So there we have God's call to four people. All four went on to become well known and willing agents in the Lord's unfolding drama of redemption. But in all four the initial responses were feelings of wonder and unworthiness. "Don't ask me Lord, I am not qualified; I am not worthy to act or speak in your name. I am inadequate. I am not a sufficiently holy person to baptize, to preach the Word, to heal, to preside at the Eucharist. I am a sinful man."

So, what are the requirements for one to minister in the

God's Church? Or, to put it another way, how can one claim to be worthy to minister in the Lord's name?

That's an issue the church had to deal with right out of the chute. And there was a lot of disagreement around it for quite a while; in fact it lingers still. The early church did basically resolve the issue however. They held that the validity of the sacraments was not a function of the holiness or lack thereof of the presiding official. Nobody is worthy in that sense, and if the validity of the sacraments hung on the worthiness of the officiant, we'd have no sacraments. The authority operative in the sacraments is God's, not that of the officiant. In the ordination of the "Philadelphia eleven" (women who were illegally ordained by several bishops in order to get the church off center on an issue that was paralyzing us). The official word from the top was that the ordinations were "irregular" but not "invalid." It was recognized that the ordinands were truly ordained even though the service had not been properly authorized.

Contrast that with the RC position on a celibate priesthood. Celibacy was not always a requirement for priesthood. There were married priests in the early church. However there were questions about the purity or holiness of a priest experiencing sexual relations with his wife. (As though intercourse were somehow unholy or unclean.) At first this was resolved by ruling that the priest abstain from sex for some period of time prior to serving at the altar (3 days?). However another trend was on a collision course with the first one. Over time the priest was expected to celebrate the Eucharist more and more frequently until the daily Eucharist became the rule for everybody. Well, that pretty much eliminated a married priesthood. And that's where we are today. It's a shame, as celibacy is the root of so many problems in the RC church and it's a church policy with no theological basis.

Well, we do have requirements, standards one is expected to meet before ordination or licensing for particular ministries; a personal discipline of study and prayer, evidence of wholesome living-a holy life. But those are formative disciplines, meant to contribute to our growth in the faith, things associated with being a Christian and more rooted in baptism than licensing. I don't see this ordaining or licensing as "granting permission or conferring authority" for one to serve. The individual is called first. Then comes preparation, equipping for ministry. Eventually authority is recognized, not conferred. Then comes ordination or licensing.

While Lynne was running the EFM training program in Colorado, she had occasion to sponsor the mentor training events. Now and then she would register for the course herself, to keep her mentor training up to date. One year she found herself in training with a priest she had never worked with. At one point in the proceedings he, apparently moved to justify himself before the rest of the group, explained that, as priest, he was called to a higher level of spirituality or piety than mere lay people. (It's called one-upmanship.) This was an additional burden that, as priest, he was obliged to bear. Lynne would have none of that. She tore into him and ripped him up one side and down the other. I doubt if she convinced him; but a lot of the laity in attendance were listening, and probably picked up some new pointers. What was the priest claiming? That because of his greater measure of holiness, he was authorized to pronounce blessings and preside at the Eucharist? The church refuted that argument centuries ago.

So, let's reiterate: The question of authority in any ministry in church or world is not based on the worthiness of the minister. Remember Matthew's theory of authority which we visited before. All authority is God's. It is not linked to titles or roles or position or the piety of the minister. It is a function of works and becomes manifest in the action. And that, in turn is a function of the one who hears the call and responds in freedom and in faith. The response we call ministry; but the authority in it is God's.

So it is that when you hear God's call to some ministry, you are not likely to be 100% sure that you got it all right. There will be feelings of inadequacies, of unworthiness, and uncertainty of the call itself. That's to be expected–take it and go with it.

The ones who scare me are those who march forth boldly, 100% sure that they heard it all very clearly, and certain that they are doing God's will. So out they charge, banners unfurled, drums beating; confident and determined. When I see that kind, totally convinced that they are the obvious ones to deliver on God's mission, count me among the skeptics or unbelievers. No – No – Give me a Gideon or a Paul or a Peter or a Mary. I can identify with those who are not totally sure but who nevertheless say "yes!" That, I believe, is what we call faith.

October 2, 2005

REPORTING TO GOD

Stewardship

Many, many years ago, when my grandfather was a young man, he invited a gentleman friend of his to go to church with him one Sunday. The church was St. John's Episcopal Church, Sharon, PA, the church we all grew up in. At the offering my grandfather's friend accidentally put a Twenty dollar gold piece in the plate instead of the usual (for those times) quarter. An easy mistake to make considering that both would feel about the same in one's pocket. By the end of the service he realized what he had done, and nervously confided with my grandfather. "Oh that's OK" assured my grandfather. "I'll go with you back to the sacristy as soon as the congregation clears out, and we'll explain to the rector. He'll understand, and we can make the switch."

The friend felt embarrassed, very uncomfortable, and obviously reluctant at the prospects of approaching the rector. So, he stammered, stalled for a bit, then, with renewed resolve, and trying to be very nonchalant about the whole thing, he shrugged and said, "No! – I gave it to the Lord - - - - t' hell with it!"

Stewardship is a topic I've wanted to discuss with you for some time. I've preached on the subject many times. Years ago I published a Forward Day by Day tract on stewardship called "Stewards, Owners & Victims." Lynne and I created a board game for teaching stewardship. The players did not compete with one another, but cooperated in a team effort to beat the game itself. We called it En Trust. We tested it extensively and it was a huge success. But we could never get it published. The cost of production would have been too much.

Anyway, in preparation for today I looked up stewardship in the dictionary. A steward is an employee, an attendant, or a manager of a grand estate, on a cruse ship or a plane; in charge of culinary affairs, keeping the books, looking after passenger comfort etc. and reporting to a master, or a captain. Notice the two sides: responsible for some set of duties, and accountable to a superior.

Do you remember the days when a Flight Attendant on a plane was called a stewardess? Those were the days when all the folk on the flight deck were men. So, if you happen to be present when people were boarding and you saw a small group in uniform you could tell right away where they were headed. If they were male, to the flight deck; if female, to the galley. Then the airlines went and messed everything up. We started seeing men in uniform serving meals in the cabin, and women who walked right onto the flight deck and sat down at the controls.

With that, the term "Stewardess" had to go. A gender neutral label was needed–so, "flight attendant." But perspectives as well as titles change. I suppose the image of a stewardess tending to culinary affairs or the comfort of passengers works in most people's minds. But that image is forever changed for me.

I was in an aisle seat on the right side of the cabin. The meal had been served to most passengers, and people were digging in when I noticed a guy in a window seat across the aisle and a row ahead of me choking and turning blue. The stewardess spotted it about the same time. But she flew into action; two big guys directly across from me were thrown out of their seats, food and food trays flew every which way; she dove into the space behind the distressed passenger, reached over the seat back, locked her arms around his chest and forcefully dislodged something that had stuck in his windpipe. She saved his life, and I hardly knew what was going on. That gave me a new perspective on the duties of a flight attendant.

Well, let's come back to our definition. A steward is one who is responsible for something, (duties, chores, etc.) and accountable to a master. As Christian stewards we have some responsibility for everything around us; our home or apartment; our check book; our car, if we have one. Then we hold various corporate responsibilities on behalf of each other. For example this plant; the building, the grounds, the equipment; our services of worship, our outreach, the meals we enjoy together. Some of those responsibilities we share by working together on them, some, by taking turns. But that's not the important point here. The important point here is perspective. Like my experience on that plane. When I see a flight attendant today, I don't see a dowdy culinary special- ist, I see an angel in white saving lives. It's like looking into the offering basin into which everyone has been placing quarters and, when it gets to me, seeing it full of twenty dollar gold pieces. It's all about perspectives, and it's the "reporting to God" part that gives perspective.

We had a work day last spring; you all turned out, and we got some help from others. That was not a simple matter of picking up some trash, pulling weeds, and touching up the paint. No! For those reporting to God, it was a matter of refurbishing a Grand Estate.

We approved a grant of $300 dollars to help Billie get through this special year. Well, it's not all that much. But, for people reporting to God, that's gold, frankincense and myrrh heaped on Christ's altar.

This little facility set on the edge of campus is an ocean going liner to people reporting to God.

That meal we can smell shaping up out there in our dumpy little kitchen is a twelve course banquet being prepared in our galleys, to people reporting to God.

Several years ago our national church sponsored a gathering of some sort for young people. They came up with this slogan, "be- fore every human being there go 10,000 angels crying, 'Make way for the image of God.'" It's perspective.

All the people we share living quarters with, go to school with, meet in the shop or on the street, they are all treasured, pre- cious children of God, each with an escort of 10,000 angels crying "make way for the image of God," to those reporting to God.

So, there we have it; just think of yourself as a flight attendant on this journey called The Kingdom of God, escorted by thousands of angels, responsible for some set of duties, and reporting to God. It's the "reporting to" part that really loads it up with spe- cial meaning. Enjoy the trip!

BEYOND THE WATER

Baptismal Covenant III

Every time I officiate at a baptism I feel like we are reliving the drama of Moses and the children of Israel as they depart from Egypt. In fact, when we pray the prayers of the people, which on this occasion is the Prayers for the Candidates, I get the feeling that we are praying a prayer that Moses originally prayed for the Children of Israel as they began their 40 year trek headed for the promised land. I can just hear him reciting these petitions for them as we do for our candidates. See what kinds of images of Moses and his people they conger up for you as I repeat them once more. Pay special attention to the verbs: deliver, open, fill, keep, teach, send, bring. We are really praying for God's action, as, I can imagine, Moses did. "Deliver them, O Lord, from the way of sin and death."

This is a jurisdiction issue. Where do we live? Whose are we? Before Moses could begin his march to the Promised Land he had to convince Pharaoh to turn the people loose; set them free. It took a lot of convincing. As we begin our journeys in faith, we are prisoners of sin and death. So the first step is to break the bonds that enslave us. For Moses the cry was "Let my people go!" For us it is "Deliver us from the way of sin and death." The early Christians were called "The people of the Way." So, we too can be called the people of the way. But the way of sin and death is the wrong way. "Open their hearts to your grace and truth."

The image I get here is that of the produce department in a grocery store. You walk into that space, look around sort of taking stock of things, get some ideas, then, head for that big roll of plastic bags. You tug at the roll to get one free, then a snap of the wrist to rip it off. But the plastic is so thin and so clingy it's a big struggle to get the bag open. So you massage it this way with your fingers, then that way. Then, if you can get just a little gap,

bring it up to your lips and try blowing into it. Well, you can't get
the good stuff into it if you can't get the bag open. So too with
our candidates, and, I suppose, with Moses' people. We pray that
their hearts be open to God's grace and truth. "Fill them with
your holy and life-giving Spirit."

Assuming that we were successful in opening their hearts, now
it's time to fill them up. Holy means whole, complete, dedicated, useful. Holy needs a "to" to be complete, as in "useful to,"
"dedicated to" and the implied subject is God; "useful to God,"
"dedicated to God." "Life-giving Spirit" is nearly a redundancy.
Spirit means life. It also means breath, wind, as in "Breathe on
me, Breath of God, fill me with life a-new . . ." So, our prayer
here is that God powerfully take over the lives of these candidates, that they be totally dedicated to the service of God. I'm
sure that would work for Moses too.

"Keep them in the faith and communion of your holy Church."

Faith has been called the substance of culture, the content,
that which gives it its character. The Christian faith is summed up
in the creeds. And, of course, we recite the Apostle's Creed on
nearly every occasion of public worship. In this way we are forming ourselves into the substance of the creed – building Christian
character. Moses didn't have anything quite like the creeds when
he pulled off his rescue in Egypt, but I think he recognized the
need. Once they were on their way and as soon as he got on top
of that mountain, the revelation came to him, and he came down
the mountain with the Decalogue. In Hebrew culture, that would
be the equivalent of the creed; the substance of culture. Communion is a community-shared common faith. (The Episcopal Church
is a Christian Communion.) Here we pray that God keeps us in
the faith and communion of his holy Church. "Teach them to love
others in the power of the Spirit."

Remember the song from the musical "Miss Saigon," "You
have to be taught to hate someone?" The setting is, of course,
Vietnam. The G.Is are lonely, longing for home, and experiencing some cultural tension with the Vietnamese. It's the cultural
friction that gives rise to the song. According to the lyrics, preju-
dice is not natural, it has to be learned. I think that's right. Tiny
children of all cultures and races can be mixed up with no trou-

ble, until someone points out that they are different. "You have to be taught to hate someone; you have to be carefully taught." That, however, is the way of sin and death. Our intention is to go a different way. So, we pray to God to teach us to love others in the power of the Spirit. And we travel the way of truth and love. "Send them into the world in witness to your love."

To be sent is to be given an assignment that takes us a-field, to be sent out, as a messenger, or an ambassador-we are sent into the world. But what's the message? We are sent out to witness to God's love. What are the ways we can witness? Well, we can talk and hope they will listen. We might demonstrate or show. That's a little harder to do but probably more effective. The trick is to come up with an action that really will communicate God's love. I don't think this can be staged. About all that is left is to truly be ambassadors of God's love and let it show up where it will. But that requires an ambassador who is not just a messenger but a true disciple. "Bring them to the fullness of your peace and glory."

Here we have another jurisdiction issue. Back where we started I put two questions before you: Where do we live? And, whose are we? At that point the implied response was "the way of sin and death." And we prayed to be delivered from that way. From there we prayed to be opened, to be filled, to be kept in the faith, to be taught love, then to be sent. And now we pray to be brought. This is the reverse of the earlier one to be sent. To be sent is to move out. To be brought is to be led. There are many parallels here with the story of the children of Israel. They were called out of slavery in Egypt. They were formed into a community with a purpose on their trek in the wilderness. They were brought into the Promised Land; a land of God's power and glory. And finally they were sent out-to be a light to the nations-a priestly nation for the whole world. So, in our time and on our road we recall the story of the children of Israel as we try to understand our travels through the wilderness.

However, we must not overlook one key step in their transition from slavery into the possibility of realizing their destiny – so that they could be sent and respond to their mission – they had to get beyond that water. Their way was blocked by the Red Sea and the Egyptians were in hot pursuit with vastly superior military forces. At first it looked like they were trapped with the sea in front of them and the Egyptians at their heels. But Moses simply led them through the sea to dry land on the other side. Their real mission and their true calling could then begin on the other side of the water. So, we too lead our baptismal candidates through the water of baptism, knowing that the real Christian adventure, the glory, the fun, excitement and joy, is about to unfold before them, their story of a full life in Christ will be experienced on the journey beyond the water of baptism.

ALL IS NOT RELATIVE

Relative and Ultimate Concerns

Give then to the emperor the things that are the emperor's, and to God the things that are God's.

When they heard this they were amazed; and they left him and went away.

Every time I read of this incident my first response is, "Why were they amazed?" What is so amazing about Jesus' response? Sounds fair enough to me; as an American in a culture in which separation of church and state is important to our basic freedoms, Render to the emperor the things that are the emperor's and to God the things that are God's. Well, of course! Why the amazement?

Well, let's examine this account a little more closely. The Pharisees, we are told right up front, have plotted to entrap Jesus. So, they send their disciples (representing the Jewish establishment) and some Herodians (representing Rome) to set the trap. They begin by trying to butter him up, "We know that you are sincere and teach the way of God in accordance with the truth, and show deference to no one." Then the loaded question: "Is it lawful to pay taxes to the emperor or not?" If Jesus says "yes" the Jews will consider him a traitor to Israel. If he says "no" the Herodians will hear that as disloyalty to Rome.

So, Jesus asks to see the coin that is used for the tax. "Whose head is this?" The Greek word is "eikon" A better translation is "image." Whose image is this? They say "the emperor's." "Then give to the emperor the things that are the emperor's, and to God the things that are God's."

Matthew's audience would pick up on a play on words here that we don't hear in the English translation. Matthew's hearers knew the Hebrew Scriptures, and in the creation narratives we are told that God created humanity in God's image. The emperor's image on the coin is of little consequence to Matthew's people – they don't belong to the emperor. But they do belong to God; they are created in God's image. The issue here is not taxes. It's the very identity of the people. Who are they? Whose are they? Jesus saw this immediately and without arguing, nailed it down; and "They were amazed!"

Consider with me, if you will, the distinction between relative and ultimate concerns or commitments. If it is a matter of relative importance–that is, if the concern is more or less important relative to other concerns–we are faced with weighing, judging, compromising and deciding just how important this matter is alongside other matters to which we also have conditional commitments.

I once prepared a paper for our national church on ways priorities could be measured in the budgeting process. To illustrate, I used the family budget. Let's say a certain family budgets 35% of its income for housing and 10% for its church pledge. That's one way of discerning priorities; it tells us that housing is three and a half times more important than church support. But that's not really fair. Housing in our world is, by nature, a high-priced category. So, let's come at it another way; by looking at how the family administers that budget. If, in times of budget surplus, the church budget is generously supplemented, and if, in times of hardship, the church pledge is zealously guarded from erosion, one might conclude that the church pledge is indeed a high priority. Well, we all do something like this with our priorities, don't we? Yet in all of this, we are looking at concerns of relative importance.

These are not ultimate, absolute, or unconditional concerns. When we look at things of relative importance, we must weigh, compromise, consider trade-offs, and make judgments, and church pledges are part of that. But when we come face to face with the object of our ultimate concern, our unconditional, absolute loyalty, we are in a whole different place. No weighing, no trade-offs, no compromises with that which is absolute and ultimate. We stare into the depths in awe and fear, captured by it, consumed by it, engulfed in it. You see, Jesus is certainly not saying, "Well, consider the relative importance of Rome, and of the Kingdom, weigh and balance, and make a well reasoned judgment about the matter." Yet that's the way this encounter is usually understood. No, I would paraphrase Jesus' response along these lines: "Go ahead and pay the stupid tax and keep yourselves out of trouble. But your soul, your life, your very being belongs to God. And you don't compromise that." And that's the difference between relative and ultimate commitments.

Sometimes life faces us with some very difficult choices, and sometimes those choices have something to do with what is relative and what is of ultimate importance. And, on occasion, Jesus himself spoke some tough words about such times. "For I have come to set a man against his father, and a daughter against her mother, and a daughter-in-law against her mother-in-law . . . He who loves father or mother more than me is not worthy of me. . . .He who finds his life will lose it, and he who loses his life for my sake will find it." (Matt 10: 34ff) "I have come to bring fire to the earth–not peace, but division!" (Lk 12: 49ff) Jesus is talking about the inevitable results of his interventions, not about intended results.

Back in the early 70s I had a long term contract with the Diocese of Bethlehem in eastern PA. In those days I was quite active in the Cursillo movement. I guess I must have served on some 15 retreat teams. Also, in those days, Cursillo was very ecumenical. We (Episcopalians) got it from the Roman Catholics, and we, in turn, passed it along to the Moravians, and most retreats, sponsored by any church, had a mix of people in the leadership roles. That's how it happened that I ran into a certain Filipino priest. He had come into this country for some advanced theological education and then had stayed on. He wound up in the Roman Catholic Diocese of Allentown also in eastern PA, where his bishop had assigned him to a Puerto Rican congregation, thinking, apparently, Filipino – Puerto Rican – same difference. The poor fellow had to go take a crash course in Spanish in order to be able to properly relate to his people. But, he did, and by the time I met him, he was well established in his new community.

In any case, at one point we found ourselves on the same team. In the Cursillo design, lay-people are in charge and clergy are considered resources. Clergy are counselors in the event something of a pastoral nature comes up, and they are the theologians, responsible for certain assigned meditations and for a series of talks on the sacraments. There were two of us serving as chaplains for this particular retreat. So we divided up the chaplain's duties. And in this context I heard the Filipino priest's story. He was addressing the candidates in one of our formal talks.

It seems he was raised in a family of reasonable means and considerable ambition. His earliest aspiration was to be a priest. A call had come to him early and strong. However, his father persistently discouraged him. "No, you'll never be a priest. "Over my dead body you'll be a priest."

Through his school years the call persisted, but so did his father, "Why don't you make something of yourself? You could become a doctor or a lawyer; you don't want to throw your life away on priesthood." But the call wouldn't quit. Then he found himself in high school and he would soon have to decide. He knew what he had to do, the call was clear. But his father had lost patience. "Over my dead body you'll go to seminary!" At this point, the priest shifted his weight; he looked down at his feet, as in sad recollection. He said, "Then my father had a heart attack and dropped dead." He lifted his head, quietly surveyed the assembly and continued, "And over my father's dead body I went to seminary."

ANGLICAN SPIRITUALITY

Materialistically Considered

In popular culture there is a theological theme or quality that, otherwise normal people tend to ogle over or find awesome, but they (I venture to say) can't define in terms that would make sense to us. Yet this quality or condition is assumed to be good, positive, desirable; an unexamined assumption. The condition I have in mind is "spirituality." This afternoon I'm going to talk about Anglican Spirituality–that is, spirituality as understood and expressed in the Episcopal Church. And let me say right up front that I don't have much use for the good press that popular spirituality gets in the Episcopal Church and elsewhere. So, I'm out to take down that positive fiction and set before you a spirituality that will stand up to tough theological scrutiny, make sense to you, and have credibility wherever we express it.

The basic error in popular spirituality is in the way it relates itself to good and evil. According to this popular view anything "spiritual" as in person, or book, you name it, is good. Anything physical, corporeal, is, at least prone to evil. That part of the popular case is exactly backwards. There is nothing morally wrong with your bodies. You may have injuries, bruises, allergies, but those are health issues, not issues of morality. Basically your bodies are strong, fit, beautiful, but, again, those are matters of physical, not moral conditioning. It's our spiritual side, our spirituality that gets us into moral trouble. It's the spirit that tempts us, that leads us astray, that brings on jealousy, envy, covetousness, anger and so on. It's our spiritual side that exposes us to guilt; indeed, that heaps guilt upon us. In popular culture "spirituality" is under examined, not understood and, in general, misrepresented.

Now, having disavowed ourselves of the idea that there is

anything innately good about spirituality, let us now proceed, unimpeded by this cultural baggage that spirituality is somehow "good," and construct a theory of spirituality that will meet the criteria that I just set up; one that has theological integrity, makes sense to you, and has credibility wherever we attempt to express it.

The first thing to be said about Anglican spirituality is that we are not Pentecostal, we are Trinitarian. We believe in the doctrine of the trinity as hammered out by the church fathers and as expressed in the creeds: three persons; one God. The terms Father, Son and Spirit are not to be taken too literally but as pointing to the eternal mystery and reality of the trinity. A system of theology is like a window pane. The idea is to look through it for the inspiration beyond. Taking everything too literally is like straining at the fly specs on the glass instead, and missing altogether the glorious view that the window offers.

By Father, we mean God the Creator, and as Creator, law giver. He created it–he gets to say how it works best. By God the Son we mean God Incarnate. God personally in his creation and taking on humanity even to death on the cross, and in that self sacrifice, presenting our humanity to eternal life. By God the Holy Spirit we mean God the Life Giver who came like fire and wind into the early church at Pentecost filling it with vitality and power, and sustaining it with life and guidance over all time.

Now, in our overall theologizing about these things, it is important that we maintain some balance in our treatment of the three "persons" of the Triune God. You've heard of religions that are overly harsh, mean and judgmental. God is a law giver and judge, and we are here to toe the mark. If that's all there is to it, well, pity us. That's an example of emphasizing "Father" to the neglect of the other two persons of the Godhead. We might think of the Mormons and of the Jehovah's Witnesses as modern examples of this theological emphasis; a tendency to be over zealous followers of the law with little sense of grace.

You may have run into religions that over emphasize the humanity of Jesus; Jesus our brother, Jesus our sojourner. It's an emphasis that needs to be reinserted into the mix on occasion;

it tends to get short shrift. Cursillo piety is big on the humanity of Jesus but it sometimes gets over blown to the point of being a kind of Jesus idolatry. I've gone to the Communion rail to be presented bread by the Eucharistic minister with the words, "Body of Jesus." I'm not there to consume the flesh of Jesus, but to participate in the Body of Christ. It's not the same thing. Jesus as Christ; Jesus as Eternal Word of God; It's the Christ of God that I hope to encounter in the Eucharist, not the Rabbi of Nazareth. In any case, balance is the key. We need the Creator and Law Giver; and we need the Word, the Christ; so also we need the element of Life Vitality.

You've probably run into the Pentecostals, those who over-emphasize the Holy Spirit to the neglect of the other Persons of the Trinity. In the extreme the Pentecostals can take the position that "God is in control of everything." (a popular bumper sticker a few years back). This can be accompanied by the conviction that I must seek God's guidance in everything I do; when to visit my dentist; where to find a parking space on a busy city block. This in turn invites an attitude of irresponsibility, resignation, or inevitability: "It was God's will," "God made me do it," "God called her home," "God will take care of it." I once served on a committee with Bishop Wolfrum when the subject of God's guidance came up. He remarked that the only time in his life when he could say that he literally heard the voice of God was once when faced with a difficult decision. He had prayed about it several times. Finally, when praying about it yet again, he heard the voice very distinctly, "Wolfrum, when are you going to quit waffling, make a decision, and get on with it?" God is not in control of everything. He gave me a brain and free will; I can't abdicate everything that comes my way. And so it is that we are not Pentecostal, but Trinitarian.

The next point to be made about Anglican Spirituality is that we are not Spiritualists but Sacramentalists. The question we encounter here is "what is real?" Christian Science, for example denies the reality of anything physical. Physical illness is an illusion. Never mind trying to cure the body; just get it out of your head. Anglicanism, on the other hand has been called the most materialistic of all religions. I like that. I praise God for our senses that make it possible to experience the world around us. For our vision and the glorious colors of a sunset; for our hearing and the grand experience of Handel's Messiah and other great music that tears at our hearts. For the sweet smell of freshly cut grass, or bread just out of the oven, for the luscious taste of a Colorado peach; for the fine texture and smoothness of a baby's bottom. All of these experiences are not merely physical, they are also spiritual and that's what makes life sacramental. A sacrament is an outward and visible sign of an inward and spiritual grace. We are created sacramental. The way we interact with each other isn't merely physical, not merely spiritual it is both; A hug, a kiss, making love, holding hands, breaking bread and sharing, a baptism; what could be more natural? Is it any wonder that we are constantly creating new sacraments? Consider a child's birthday party; note the parallels with the Eucharist. The people gather at some appointed time bearing gifts. The liturgy will probably include games and singing. Then, of course, the high point, the candles are blown out, and the one in whose honor we are gathered cuts the cake and passes it around. If Aunt Jane can't be there, we'll cut a special piece and take it to her. Reserved sacrament at a birthday party is appropriate too. God, who is spirit has chosen to meet us sacramentally, how deliciously appropriate; how natural. How else?

The next thing to note about Anglican Spirituality is that we are not subjects of an iron-fisted ruler; we are not slaves, but partners with the Almighty. That partnership agreement is called a covenant. God invites us into this agreement. In our freedom, we can accept or refuse. God has not predetermined how everything in his creation is going to work out in the end. Partnership means that we are co-creators with God. God created plants to be, well, plants. God created animals to be, well, just animals. But he created humans to be, partners. He didn't know what we might do or become at the outset. And God might have set himself up for some grave disappointments and for some delightful surprises. How was he to know? But whatever our contribution, he can redeem it. We are in it together, to the end.

So, as Anglicans, our spirituality is not Pentecostal but Trinitarian. We are not Spiritualists but Sacramentalists; we are not slaves but partners. As Anglicans, spirituality is expressed in our freedom, our appreciation of the created order and our knowledge that we are on an adventure that is loaded with meaning, destined for glory and we journey in the company of our partner, the Almighty. Now, that's some adventure!

HEARING AND SEEING

Christmas 2005

There is seeing and then there is "Seeing." There is seeing as in 20-20 vision. And there is seeing as in comprehending. And the two often do not go together. These two seeings are part of everyday discourse. "Can't you see that?" Or, simply "See?" "Well, I don't see that at all!" "Do you get it?" I can watch a soccer game, but I don't see a game–just a lot of apparent aimless activity.

Similarly, there is hearing, and then there is "Hearing." One might hear the words without grasping the message. "Now, listen to what I'm saying!" "Do you get the drift?" "What you are saying makes absolutely no sense to me." I can listen to some kinds of contemporary music, but all I hear is noise. One of Luke's favorite literary devices is playing with the double meanings of words such as seeing and hearing. So, in Luke we frequently run into leaders, educated or highly placed people, sometimes "the crowds" and often the disciples who see but do not see; who hear, but do not hear. Then we have the lowly, the stranger, the outsider, the simple, uneducated, even the blind who see and hear.

Take Luke's account of the crucifixion for example; consider the cast of characters in light of who's hearing and seeing what. First there are the crowds–the very crowds who, a little earlier, were calling for his death; "Crucify Him!" Now, while their leaders scoff at him, they mill around having second thoughts about what they have done. If he is the messiah he shouldn't be here. So they watch but do not see. After it is all over, Luke tells us, "They returned home, beating their breasts."

Then we have Jesus' followers who, "stood at a distance watching these things."

The image I get here is one of a small herd of cattle where there is a fracas of some sort in the pasture. They stand motionless at a distance and watch. They are not frightened enough to run, and not curious enough to come closer. So they stand there stupidly watching but not comprehending. That, I think is Luke's portrayal of Jesus' followers.

Then we have those two criminals also nailed up there. One of them derides Jesus, "So, you're the messiah, save yourself–and us!" But the second one "gets it." "Oh shut up!" he tells his part-ner in crime, "We're just getting what we deserve–but this man is innocent." Then he turns to Jesus, "Remember me when you come into your kingdom."

Soldiers also scoffed at him: Gave him vinegar to drink, cast lots for his clothes while he hung there naked. But at the very end revelation came to one centurion. Luke says that "When he saw what had taken place, he praised God and declared Jesus in-nocent." So, neither Jesus' followers nor the crowds, nor anyone there heard or saw what was going on–except for two outsiders, a dying criminal and a lonely soldier.

Now, in a similar way, let us examine the Christmas Gospel. See the cast of characters–what did they hear and see? First there is Emperor Augustus. He had just called for a census–a big one–the whole world. There was the usual argument in the Senate; whether it would be an actual head count or some kind of statis-tical projection. But the Republicans won; it would be an actual head count. That's why everybody had to go back to their home town.

Augustus' real name was Octavian. In those days it was com-mon to attribute divine qualities to the leader, and not infre-quently the leader claimed such. Octavian was known as a good leader and called, "The August One;" so, the title, "Emperor Augustus." Luke is, here, setting us up for a little irony–which I'll point out later. In any case, we have Augustus and Gover-nor Quirinius who, in Luke's account, are oblivious to the whole story–which is part of the irony.

Then we have the messenger, an angel of the Lord, bringing the revelation. But to whom? Well, not to the Emperor or the Governor; they don't know anything about the prophecies. Not to Mary and Joseph; they probably would not be able to hear and see, and even if they could, who would believe them? Two kids with an illegitimate child–who are they making themselves out to be? Not to the religious establishment–all those highly placed and well educated Pharisees, Sadducees, lawyers and teachers. They wouldn't have ears to hear or eyes to see.

So, true to Lukan form, the angel goes to the lowly, uneducated, unsophisticated shepherds – on a hillside, in the dark of night, the only ones in the neighborhood likely to hear and see. The angel never refers to Jesus by name. He calls him Savior, Messiah or Christ, and Lord, all titles that could be applied to Augustus. And therein lies the irony. As the Savior comes into the world, the one who thinks he's savior and all his officials are ignorant of the whole thing.

But, continuing our cast of characters, "And suddenly there was with the angel a multitude of the heavenly host praising God and saying, Glory to God in the highest heaven." That should settle it for the shepherds if they had any doubt.

So they said to one another, "Let us go now to Bethlehem and see this thing that has taken place." So they went with haste and found Mary and Joseph, and the child lying in the manger. "When they saw this, they made known what had been told them." We don't know what Joseph made of all this but Luke gives us a clue about Mary who "treasured all these words and pondered them in her heart." And, we are told, the shepherds "returned glorifying and praising God for all they had heard and seen."

Now, there are some characters in this story who can easily slip by unnoticed. Luke tells us that after the shepherds' report, "All who heard it were amazed." Who is this "all?" Who also was there on that holy night? The picture we get at first is that the shepherds found ONLY Mary, Joseph and the child in the manger. Yet this line suggests that there were others present and that they heard the message! Who were they? Well, let's redraw this picture in our mind's eye to include others who were not just standing at a distance watching, but who were totally present and did hear and see. In this picture we will need, not a small cattle shed–but a real barn.

My best guess is that the others who were there on that holy night were the others who also could not find lodging at the inn; they couldn't pay for it, or were too late, or were unacceptable. With a little imagination we should be able to see them too. I can see some of them.

There is a little five-year-old crippled girl with one crutch, dressed in rags, about like the cloths that cover the baby; she seems to be alone. She is, of course drawn to the manger. Cautiously, gently, she approaches, takes Jesus' hand into her own. He smiles at her; she turns to the crowd, face beaming.

And here is an old grandmother from Emmaus. Got here just in time to help Mary with the delivery; tore off some of her own clothes to clean and then wrap the baby. Now she hovers over Mary and child like they were hers.

I see a tax collector up from Jericho; a man despised by everyone, alone and lonely. But in a way, he's at home in this crowd of castoffs.

There's a young couple with a three-month-old baby. They immediately feel a kinship with Mary and Joseph. And the four of them busily share experiences and admire babies.

And there is this old dock hand up from Joppa–been kicked around and abused for years. But every day he faithfully goes to the synagogue to pray for the Messiah to come soon.

Now see, we too are present. In Word and Sacrament, in liturgy and in music we are present . . . in that barn. Not merely watching, but totally present with the others. Then in come the shepherds–expectant, excited, awe struck. We can see it in their faces. They share their message as it had been told them. We are all amazed at what they have to say. Later, it's time for us to go. We leave glorifying and praising God for all we have heard and seen.

February 10, 2006   Epip. 7:Lk.24; 3ff

TRAVELING TO EMMAUS

Of Meaning and Purpose

Back in November of last year I was doing some advance work on a sermon that I never preached. The subject was Meaning and Purpose and I even had a title for it, Traveling to Emmaus. Then tragedy came into my life, and I laid the draft, nearly finished, aside. I think it is now time to take it up again. I'll read it so you will get it as I left it three months ago.

Some 2000 years ago on Easter Day, a couple of guys set off on foot from Jerusalem headed for the village of Emmaus, seven miles or so to the west. It must have been about mid-afternoon. We are not told why they wanted to get to Emmaus; just that Emmaus was their destination. That they were long in the face as they quietly reviewed their recent experience is understandable. They had just, a couple of days earlier, witnessed the torturous murder of their leader, one in whom they had placed such high hopes. And to further confuse things, certain women of their group were now circulating stories to the effect that he was not really dead. As they walked, a stranger joined them and tried to pick up on the conversation. He was unduly curious about their sad countenance and demeanor.

As it turned out, the stranger was well versed in scripture and as the conversation developed, he was moved to give them a summary review of the message of the prophets – a sort of ad hoc Adult Bible course on the run. They were impressed, but didn't really get it. As the afternoon wore on, they arrived at the outskirts of Emmaus. The travelers from Jerusalem seemed to know where they were going, so they invited their new traveling companion to join them for the evening, which he did. Later, at the table, it was the stranger who said the blessing, broke the bread and passed it around. That's when it hit them. But when they looked again, he was gone. That did it. They got right up and high tailed it back to Jerusalem to join the others still gathered there.

Now notice this about that story:

We never did find out why those two men were going to Emmaus.

We never really found out whether they made it all the way.

It seems fairly clear that running into that stranger on the way was not part of their original plan.

But notice this also, about our reaction to the story:

Why those two journeyed to Emmaus and whether they actually made it all the way turns out to be unimportant detail. What grabs our attention is what happened along the way. This brief story gives us a very good introduction to the distinction between meaning and purpose, two words commonly used as synonyms, which they are not. In this story purpose has to do with the end (intended destination). But we soon lose track of that. Meaning has to do with what happens along the way. We don't lose track of that.

Getting to Emmaus seems to have been the goal (the objective, the intention). Or, we could say, "The travelers had a purpose," ie. getting to Emmaus. If the person, or activity, or project is aimed toward a tangible result or a new specified condition, the activity can be said to have purpose. The purpose explains the "why" of the activity. Notice this: (1) the purpose was up front, it went in before the action commenced. (2) It was of human origin. It was some body's, or some human agency's purpose.

Meaning, on the other hand, is more difficult to get a grip on. Meaning has a mystical quality to it. Meaning does not go in up front. It is often discovered in retrospect, and it seems to reflect divine not human agenda. Words have meaning. Words also have power. If the purpose or goal has been well formulated, words have the power to inspire others, so that many may be moved (inspired, infused with spirit – energy – power) to help in addressing the cause. Thus a compelling purpose might be said to have meaning for some people (those inspired) but not for all people. However the purpose will be clear to all. There are two kinds of activities that are void of purpose but loaded with meaning.

The first example of purposeless activity is play. I don't mean play a game-for then the player has an objective-to win the game. I don't mean play as physical exercise-for then the player has purpose-physical fitness. I mean pure purposeless activity; for the pure joy of it. (but if joy is the desired end, it is lost-the activity has to be goal-less to qualify as pure play) to run and romp and sing and dance for the pure joy of it. Play, in this sense, is creative. Take a scientist, a teacher, almost anyone who approaches their "work" playfully and they are likely on the road to creativity. (But creativity can't be the "purpose.") In this kind of activity the creative person loses himself-herself, in curiosity, in the pure wonder of being absorbed in the play.

Playing an instrument in an orchestra is probably a good example of what I am trying to get at. I doubt if many musicians do this for the pay involved-it's the deep satisfaction of contributing to the overall effect of many musicians playing together. Another very good example of this is a couple in love. The couple, unself-consciously, with no inhibitions and without purpose, come together in what can best be called pure play; two people completely absorbed in it. The ultimate human creative process. It's the exception that illustrates the point. I have frequently come across couples who somehow can't seem to conceive though desperately wanting a child. So they go through all kinds of disciplines to improve the odds that a pregnancy will ensue. This can go on for months, to no avail. But notice what they have done here: they have inserted the element of purpose into an act that is fundamentally play. So, it doesn't work; after a while they give up and adopt a child. This works just fine and the new family settles into their new life together. Then the woman discovers that she is pregnant. Take purpose out of the mix and creativity returns. I don't offer this as a proposed solution, only an observation.

The second is an accident or random violence triggered by a hurricane for example; or an earthquake, or an illness; or human recklessness or foolishness. Such events are, by definition, without purpose. Yet, we all know people who have been victims of such tragedy. The typical response is for the victim to sit dazed, trying to wring some purpose out of it. Since there is no human purpose in it, the grief and questions turn to God. "What was God up to here?" Since there are no easy answers and since we have an uncompromising sense of justice, the feelings turn to guilt: What am I being punished for? What did I do that was so bad? And if that's the road we're inclined to travel, we'll find some answers, we'll feel the guilt and (chances are) accept the punishment as fair. When counseling a friend in such a predicament we have to insist that they are not being punished by God. God is not angry with them. They have done nothing to deserve this. But, most important, the incident was without purpose to begin with; no human or divine purpose in there anywhere. We are vulnerable, living in an imperfect world. Such things happen. There is no word to explain it.

Yet over time, words are found (inspiration again) not words to explain the purpose, for there was no purpose-but words to explore the meaning and to redeem the event. Lives are changed and lives go on, and very often, the purposeless tragedy is found to be loaded with meaning for one's own life.

And that's as far as I got on my sermon, Traveling to Emmaus until a few days ago when it occurred to me that I'm still on that road. Not traveling TO Emmaus. I've been to Emmaus. He has revealed himself to me "in the breaking of the bread." I'm now traveling FROM Emmaus. To ? ? ? I don't know. And destinations, goals, ends don't matter. It's what happens along the way that matters.

We have this art work hanging over the head of our bed. It's been there about as long as we've been together. It's a calligraphy by artist Michael Podesta and was given to us as a wedding present by a dear friend in Alaska.

> Rich is not how much you have . . .
> Or where you are going . . .
> Or even what you are . . .
> Rich is who you have beside you.

STUPID TURTLE

Farewell Message to Canterbury House

Depart for FL 3/16/06

Note: This was my final sermon with the congregation of Canterbury House. Lynne had died January 5th. She would have been 62 on March 2nd. My own failing health called for a move away from the high altitude and fierce winds of the Wyoming inner-mountain west. Family in central Florida beckoned. It was a very difficult departure. One of my final duties in Laramie was to wrap up a class for new members that I had started. That is the context of this message.

Last Tuesday, on your behalf, I led our final session for Christian Inquirers. On a date yet to be determined, Ava, our president will present to Bruce, our bishop, a class of seven candidates for confirmation or reaffirmation of baptismal vows. I know that you will want to watch for this date, and be on hand to support these pilgrims as they take their next step in their journeys in the faith.

At our first Inquirers' session on January 10th, (The day following the day of Lynne's Memorial Service), I opened the meeting by passing this around [Lynne's Baptismal Certificate; framed and mounted] which I do once more (for this group) this afternoon:

"In the name of the Father, and the Son, and the Holy Ghost. Amen. This certifies that Lynne Elizabeth Davenport was received into the Congregation of Christ's flock by Holy Baptism on Rogation Sunday, the 14th day of May, 1944."

Lynne was two and one half months old.

When Lynne and I were married, and trying to put some order into our papers and records, I first saw this document tucked away in an old manila folder with some other stuff. It probably hadn't been looked at in years. But, somehow, over the next 20 some years, it made its way from that old file folder to this frame which, following her death, I retrieved from its very conspicuous position on her office wall. Now here is the question I ask you to speculate about: Over those years, what was going on that resulted in this scrap of paper making its way from a non-descript manila file folder to a prominent place on Lynne's office wall?

I can speculate on that question; but then I have an unfair advantage-I've lived with her over those years. However, I must say, I don't really know the specifics of how or just when this framed certificate got on her office wall. I'll just (like a little kid) point my finger and say "she did it."

I don't really know, but, like you, I can speculate. If ever there were a theme or a symbol that would characterize our joint ministries over the past 25 years, baptismal ministry, or the ministry of all the baptized, would capture the essence of it. I'm sure that the shift from the manila file folder to the office wall reflects Lynne's growing affirmation and appreciation of her own baptismal ministry. And spreading that word of the prominence of Baptismal Ministry was why she was in this diocese.

Over the two and a half years I have been with you, I have tried to emphasize to you (as part of that theme) how important, how precious, how wonderful you are. Of course God loves you and in that you are valuable beyond measure. It's not enough that you know this in your head, you must also feel the reality of it in your heart. This is often a hard reality for young people to accept; well, for any of us. We are surrounded by so much judgment, hounded by attitudes of unworthiness and guilt. People expect so much. But you have every right in the world to hold your head up high, and present yourselves to the world as valued, treasured, precious children of God, and furthermore, as Christians commissioned to minister in the Name of Christ. How can I convey to you the enormity of this truth? Well, I'll try.

The value of a thing is not a function of the innate value of the thing itself; like a treasure buried in a field or a pearl of great price hidden in a closet. No, the value of a thing resides in the heart and soul of the one who values. So when I say that you are precious beyond measure, I'm not trying to explain things in a way that would lead to big-headedness but to grateful hearts. It's not like the TV commercials asserting "you deserve it" in a ploy to get more of your money. You are precious, not because you deserve it, but because those surrounding you, including God Almighty, value you so highly. There is nothing here for you to brag about, but plenty to fill your heart with gratitude.

I think my first real insight about how valuing works came to me as a young father. Most families, I suppose, experience the trauma of loosing a pet. The dog gets hit by a car; the cat gets shot by a careless hunter; well, lots of things can happen. And it's not always an accident. Sometimes it is simply the responsible way to go, when a pet gets too old or is suffering. We've experienced our share as the kids grew up. But my first experience with this sort of thing occurred when my oldest daughter was five. I came home mid-day to find her crying inconsolably, heart broken. It turned out her pet turtle had died-you know; the kind you used to be able to buy in the five and dime store; about the size of a silver dollar. She had it in hand, and it was dead all right.

I took her in my arms and tried to comfort her. It's okay honey, we can get another. No, another wouldn't do-this was the one she loved. The sobbing continued. Fathers are supposed to be able to fix things when little girls are hurting. I held the thing in my hand-looked at it-a stupid 15 cent turtle, with a pea-sized brain. And this particular turtle of all turtles was the important one. How could such a worthless critter be causing my baby so much pain? Turtles don't even care when a turtle dies. My anger grew. I wanted to throw the damn thing on the ground and stomp on it, but I couldn't, she loved it.

I continued to hold her, but my anger was turning into fantasy. Suppose that dumb little turtle did have some sense of the rich, deep love surrounding it because of the affection of a little girl? No way! No way, that that simple creature could even have the slightest glimpse of the devastation it was causing a vastly superior being, a being capable of experiencing thousands of times more emotion, more pain, yes-more love than that insignificant, nearly brainless reptile. But I was caught in the middle and had to face reality. And the reality was the turtle was important, not because of what the turtle was, but because she loved it. Strange way to do values; importance is a function of the one valuing, not the thing valued.

My fantasy continued. Images flashed through my mind so fast it takes more time to tell about them than, initially, to experience them. I still held her; my head was somewhere else. But suppose-just suppose that little turtle could, or did, even glimpse the tiniest bit, or sense the smallest fragment of that incredible outpouring of love surrounding it. Then, I imagined the turtle trying to be "good" to justify all that tender loving affection, to earn or deserve it. Or fearful of doing something "bad" that the love might be withdrawn. Stupid turtle, I thought, nothing it could do (even if it were capable of harboring such thoughts) could possibly turn off that love. Stupid turtle! The spell was fading; then it hit me. We are all stupid little turtles. Wallowing around in this fish bowl called earth, with just the faintest glimpse, the tiniest hint of the vast love surrounding us.

And we try to lead "good" lives so we can feel like we deserve all that love; like we are worthy of it. And we try to obey all the rules, so as not to give offense that the love might be withdrawn. Stupid turtles; that we could do anything to cut off that love. Anything we did could only cause it to blossom more abundantly.

Fantasy broken, I took her hand; we found some tissue paper and carefully wrapped the little critter. I got a shovel and we walked out to the garden. She held the package and I dug the hole, and together we buried a very important little turtle.